Changing Your World
One Diaper at a Time

Marla Taviano

Blessing!

Marla Taviano

Psalm 19:14

HARVEST HOUSE PUBLISHERS

EUGENE, OREGON

Cover by Garborg Design Works, Savage, Minnesota

Cover photo © Blend Images Photography / Veer

Back cover author photo © Camille Ackerman, www.ackermanimaging.com

Marla Taviano: Published in association with William K. Jensen Literary Agency, 119 Bampton
Court, Eugene, Oregon 97404

CHANGING YOUR WORLD ONE DIAPER AT A TIME
Copyright © 2008 by Marla Taviano
Published by Harvest House Publishers
Eugene, Oregon 97402
www.harvesthousepublishers.com

Library of Congress Cataloging-in-Publication Data
    Taviano, Marla, 1975-
    Changing your world one diaper at a time / Marla Taviano.
        p. cm.
    ISBN-13: 978-0-7369-2318-7
    ISBN-10: 0-7369-2318-7
    1. Mothers—Religious life. 2. Newborn infants I. Title.
    BV4529.18.T38 2008
    248.8'431—dc22
                                                                    2007045427

Printed in the United States of America

        08 09 10 11 12 13 14 15 16 / VP-SK / 12 11 10 9 8 7 6 5 4 3 2

Contents

Down Mommy Road

As a little girl, I played with baby dolls for hours. I held them, changed them, bathed, fed them. I even pulled up my shirt (or untied one of my sundress straps) so they could "nurse" from my flat little-girl chest. One side stored milk, the other orange juice.

Who you are as a child—you in your purest sense—says a lot about the woman you'll someday become. I had a lot of ambitions when I was younger (I wanted to be a librarian, for one), but my aspiration to be a mommy trumped them all. That desire is hardwired into most of us women. We have an innate desire to play the mommy role in real life.

And then one fine day, your lifelong dream becomes a living, breathing reality.

The First Day of the Rest of Your Life

You gaze in awe at the tiny, sleeping bundle in your arms. You stroke her soft, dimpled cheek and lean down and kiss her miniature rosebud lips. Her breath is so rhythmic, so warm.

You finger her tiny hospital bracelet. You unwrap her blanket so you can stare at her miniature little toes.

You wait for the full impact of your new reality to hit you, but hours later, it still hasn't sunk in. That thin, hazy layer of fog hovers over your brain. Each moment of this day has been surreal.

I'm a mommy, you say to yourself, mouthing the words without sound. Then a whisper—"I'm a mommy."

I had a baby. I gave birth. This is my *baby. I am her mommy. She came from inside of me. She is mine.*

I am a mommy. *My life is complete. And perfect.*

We Interrupt This Lovely Scene...

You know what's coming, don't you? I'm going to set the scene for motherly bliss and then—bam!—I'll hit you upside the head with the cold, hard truth. I'm going to tell you how awful your life is about to become, how you'll rue the day you decided to conceive a child.

Relax, friend. I'll do nothing of the sort. Your life will *not* be awful as soon as you get home from the hospital. (That part comes a couple weeks later.)

What? Did no one tell you about the postpartum honeymoon? It's a similar deal to that vacation getaway after your wedding—well, minus the exotic locale. And the sex.

But it's still a honeymoon compared to what's coming.

Where Were We?

How could your new little baby be one week old already? His life is flying by! If only you could stop the hands of time!

Could there *be* a more perfect baby on the face of God's green earth? After all you'd read and heard, you had braced yourself for the exhausting life of a new mother, but you're still on cloud nine.

Your baby is behaving like an angel. He eats, burps, pees, and poops like a champion. He whimpers only when he's hungry, and he immediately stops when the source of nourishment touches his lips.

He sleeps all the time. Even in the middle of the night you look forward to hearing his sweet cry because it signals more bonding time with your cuddly cherub. What's a little sleep compared to your darling baby?

You can feel your love for him swelling up and flowing through your veins, spilling out all over the place. Your heart literally aches with love. You want to store up these moments for the rest of forever.

Your transition to motherhood has been as smooth as cheesecake. The 32-hour labor, botched epidural, and 12 stitches have long been forgotten. Sure, there's some blood and soreness. And yeah, your bra is bursting at the seams.

But your family and friends are showering you with gifts and praises and offers to do dishes and laundry. You've turned into a local hero of sorts. You had a *baby!* You haven't gotten this much attention since your wedding day.

This is the life. This is what you were born to do.

And Then You Wake Up

Beep! Beep! Beep! Beep! Beep! Beep!

What's that obnoxious sound? Why, that's your alarm clock. Rise and shine, my friend! The honeymoon's over!

Where's the snooze button?

Sorry, sweetie, those days are over too. Sleeping in is a thing of the past. You're a *mommy* now.

Remember that fateful eve many months ago when you, God, and hubby made a baby? Remember the elation of finding out you were pregnant, the miracle of feeling a real-live baby moving and growing in your belly, the euphoric dreams of the promise motherhood holds?

Unfortunately, much like our visions of wedded bliss, our dreams of becoming mothers tend to be romanticized. We drool over baby catalogs, decorate our posh nurseries, pick out scrumptious little outfits (and fold and refold them), and daydream about cuddling our angelic newborns.

Somewhere in the back of our minds, we must have some idea that motherhood isn't all peaches and cream, but we push those thoughts far, far away.

A baby of my very own to love and hold and smell and kiss and nurse and keep forever and ever. Life will be calm, complete, peaceful—in the words of the lovely Mary Poppins, "practically perfect in every way."

When real life hits, the jolt we experience is more than disconcerting; it's downright world-rocking. It doesn't take us long to figure out that babies don't come from Pottery Barn.

Our daydreams of marriage and motherhood are always idealistic, always utopic, always perfect. And why wouldn't they be? Who imagines bad things, hard things? We close our eyes and picture lovely scenarios that come together like something out of a fairy tale. And we feel so warm and fuzzy inside.

And then, for some reason, we intelligent women who really should know better think that dream equals real life. We check our common sense at our IKEA-furnished nursery doors.

And then comes the wake-up call.

The exhaustion catches up with us. Hubby goes back to work, Mom goes home. The gifts stop piling up. The laundry doesn't. The baby no longer sleeps twenty hours a day. He cries for ten instead. You're still bleeding, you hurt, and you're emotional, bursting into tears at the drop of a hat.

And what's more, you're scared. Scared to leave your baby. Scared of SIDS. Scared of bad people and monsters. Scared that you don't know how to raise a child. Scared she'll grow up to hate you and rebel. Scared that something you do wrong now will scar him for life.

You weren't cut out for this. You're a failure. You can't do this. You just can't.

The Mother of All Paradoxes

But you can. You *can* do this. You *can* be a mommy—and a good one. You can be a mom whom your child someday rises up and calls blessed.

You just can't do it on your own. You need support from your fellow humans—other moms in particular. And you need the power of the Holy Spirit, the very essence of the living God inside of you. That power already dwells within you if you've accepted Christ as your

Savior. You just have to learn to walk in Him so you can draw from that Spirit-strength.

Motherhood is the Great Tension, for lack of a better term. It's the ugly and the beautiful, the blissful and the chaotic, the fulfilling and the frustrating, the empowering and the unnerving, all rolled into one.

In this book, I attempt to walk that fine line between complete honesty and ungrateful griping. The last thing I want to do is complain, believe me, but telling you that the mommy life is a bed of petunias would be a disservice to us all.

Just know that regardless of what I say in these next couple of hundred pages or so, I know beyond balderdash that I am blessed. God is so good. He looked down on that six-year-old mommy with boobies full of orange juice and smiled. Then nearly 20 years later, He saw fit to start blessing her with real babies—and beautiful ones at that.

The story has come full circle. That six-year-old is now thirty-one with a seven-year-old of her very own. And two younger ones besides.

It just takes my breath away.

The Balance Beam

And that's what I want this book to do. To take our breath away for a bit. To remind us why we're here—why we do what we do and why it's so stinkin' important. And to inspire us with confidence that we really can do it—and do it well.

A few months ago, a woman e-mailed me regarding my book *Is That All He Thinks About?*

She said she loved the book, laughed till she cried, thought the marriage advice was godly and biblical...but thought I made children sound more like a burden than a blessing. My thoughts on motherhood made her exhausted. She has four kids under four and never gets as tired as I described. She said being a mommy teaches us to be selfless. No need to play the martyr and whine about our sacrifice.

She had read my blog and could tell I loved my children. She just wished I hadn't portrayed motherhood as a burden.

"Sorry, I know this probably sounds critical," she said, "but it hurts to see the way motherhood is made out to be a chore we must put up with until they are out of the house."

Please hear me, dear reader. I do *not* see motherhood as a chore, a burden, an inconvenience. I am *not* longing for the day when my children are grown and out of my hair. I love my little girls for all I'm worth, and I can't bear the thought of them getting big and independent and leaving the nest. I have wanted to be a mommy as long as I can remember. I mean, come on, I had orange-juice boobies 25 years ago!

In my mind, nothing is more fulfilling or rewarding than motherhood. Nothing. And I honestly believe the highest calling in all of life is to raise children to be godly adults.

However, I do not think being a mom is easy. Not by any stretch. I do not breeze through each day, thinking, *My, how effortless it is to be unselfish and give of myself unceasingly to my family! My, how much energy I have! My, what a wonderful mother I am! What an example I am to the world!*

I submit that you can be 100 percent dedicated to your family and love being a mom and still struggle with the many issues I'll address in this book. And we're only going to make it through the first short year of being a mommy!

If you are a perfect mother, put down the book. If you think motherhood is a cakewalk, just keep walking. I love you, I do, but I can't relate to you.

As for me and my house, I simply refuse to paint a rosy picture of motherhood without telling the whole truth. I must share from my heart and bare my soul, letting you see my faults and weaknesses. Only then can I truly be an encouragement to you.

Optimistic but realistic at the same time. Full of hope, yet not full of baloney. I pray that I can find the balance that will best serve you, my friend.

The Book in a Nutshell

This book isn't a how-to. It's not a developmental handbook. It's not a lecture, a guilt trip, or even an expert's opinion. And since my cousin Kyla thinks all parenting books are a snooze-fest, let me go ahead and promise that it won't be one of those either!

Think pep rally. Think fight song. Think "Go, team, go!" Encouragement and support are my bottom line. Heads nodding in understanding, belly laughs in all the right places—that's what I'm going for.

Let's be honest—parenting books are a dime a dozen. So something has to set this one apart for you and make you glad you took the time to read it. How about if I promise it'll be honest? And yeah, funny now and again too.

In my humble opinion, a book like this isn't worth the paper it's printed on if it isn't real—and if it doesn't make you crack a smile every other page or so (even laugh out loud every so often). We'll dip into the solemn and the serious, but let's have us a bit of fun too, shall we?

I'm hoping this book will put a little spring in your step, a little wind in your sails, a little glide in your stride. That it will nudge you toward the best life you and your new little family can have. That you'll finish it feeling energized, invigorated, and refilled.

Read it on the toilet (where I do my best perusing), in the doctor's office, on the treadmill, or while feeding your baby. Read it in bits and pieces or all in one sitting (just let the nanny mind the wee one).

Pull it off the shelf whenever you need a reminder that life is precious, your children are a blessing, motherhood is valuable, and each day is a gift. When you need reassurance that together, you and God can conquer the world—parenting included.

Just so we're clear on something: I'm not perfect. And I'm not naive enough to think I can please everyone. I have many questions and very few answers. Many days I feel about as qualified to be a mom as a six-year-old nursing a baby doll.

But I incessantly pray that the Holy Spirit will fill me as I write and that He will infuse my words with wisdom, grace, and hope. And, of course, wit. I do love a good dose of wit.

I like my books to feel like we're having a heart-to-heart chat. So, scootch over and make room for me on your couch. Even the rug will do!

I've brought a lot of friends along. You'll get to meet them in the following pages, and I just know some of them will be your bosom friends by the end.

My hope and prayer is that you will walk away feeling refreshed, emboldened, and inspired. This book is *for* you and *about* you, my newly mommied friend! And it's fat free, calorie free, and even gluten free, so forget about your leftover preggo weight for a few hours and eat it up!

The Beginning of Baby

1

Baby in the Works

Because you're reading this book, chances are you already have a little one in tow. But we're going to back up just a bit before we talk about actual real-live babies.

Maybe you're pregnant with your first child at this very moment. Congratulations, Mama! But let's back up even further than that.

Every woman's journey to pregnancy is different. And no, I don't mean the trip Mr. Sperm takes to pay the conjugal visit to Ms. Egg. That's pretty standard (with a few exceptions). I'm talking about the weeks, months, and years before the big conception party.

We're going to start our conversation at a time when that little baby of yours is just that—a conversation. An idea in your head.

Let me begin by asking you a question: What's the plan, Stan? Yes, I know your name is probably not Stan. In fact, I can almost guarantee it's not.

But the question is still directed at you. Do you have a plan? A plan for your life? A plan for a family? A plan for your future kids (right down to their hair color and giftedness)?

Maybe your plan goes (or went) a little something like this: Girl meets boy. They fall in love. Get engaged. Married. Get to know one another for a couple years. Look in each other's eyes one day and "know that it's time." Toss the birth control, make passionate love, take a test, share the happy news.

Nine blissful months later…

Now back to our questions. Let me ask you another one. How many things in your life typically go according to plan?

I don't keep exact records, but it seems to me that very little in my life has panned out exactly as I planned it out.

Take last fall for example. I planned a delightful vacation in the Smoky Mountains for our little family of five. I planned a romantic stay in a cozy cabin with lots of hikes up peaceful trails and brilliant fall foliage.

I did *not* plan for 30-degree weather and 50 mile-per-hour winds at the top of the mountain. Baby and I sat in the van while Daddy and the two older ones froze their buns off and about got blown off a cliff.

I did *not* plan for hours of sitting in our vehicle in stopped traffic with bored, restless children as scads of tourists left their cars running in the middle of the road to photograph a family of black bears.

I did *not* plan for my ten-month-old daughter to vomit in the van all over everything, miles from our cabin, three days in succession.

After ten years of marriage, I planned to be settled in one spot and sitting financially pretty. I did *not* plan to move nine times or throw away money on cars that broke or houses we sold for less than we paid for them.

As a young girl, I had a plan in place for my future family. I would marry at 20, wait a year, have four kids by the time I was 26, and there you go. The perfect plan.

I did *not* plan on trying for eight months to get pregnant with baby number one or trying for almost a year with number three before having a miscarriage.

So how about you, friend? How are your plans coming along?

Maybe the conception of your baby came before your wedding. Not what you had planned.

Or you found out a year into marriage that your husband really didn't want children at all—and he's not budging. Not what you had planned.

Or maybe you found yourself in tears for the sixteenth month in a row because you still weren't pregnant. Not what you had planned.

Maybe your first pregnancy ended in a devastating miscarriage. Or maybe you're pregnant, but after eight months, you're still reeling from the nausea. Maybe you gave birth to your baby—a little girl—but something is wrong, terribly wrong. Not what you had planned.

Maybe your baby is healthy, but six months later, *you* aren't—not at all. The depression is still hanging over you like a thick, dark cloud. Not what you had planned.

Is God still in control?

I know He is, friend. I know it. God had (and has!) a plan for my life—and for yours! I couldn't always figure out what God was doing—maybe you can't either—but looking back, I see the pieces fitting together. And they've made something beautiful.

Starting a Family

In the olden days, family planning was a no-brainer. You got married, started sleeping together, and if the good Lord willed it, the babies started popping out sooner than later, over and over and over again until the ol' gray mare (you) up and quit.

Nowadays, for better or worse, we put a lot more thought into the whole process. When should we start a family? How should we prepare in the meantime? How many children do we want and can we afford? Which college-prep preschool should they attend?

You'll find that nearly everyone and her sister has an opinion about each one of these things. And they aren't afraid to share, no sir.

The "helpful" parenting advice starts well in advance of the birth of your first child. Shoot, don't be surprised if it starts way before conception. Get used to it.

These people aren't afraid to ask you all manner of personal questions. They simply have no sense of boundaries.

"When you gonna have a baby? Y'all have been married for what, eight months already? What you waitin' for? You're not gettin' any younger!"

At the other end of the spectrum are the career women who think you're out of your mind to even *consider* having a child until you've climbed the corporate ladder, invested millions in your retirement account, traveled the world, and built your dream home.

The way I look at it, only three people really matter in this huge decision when to start a family—you, your husband, and God. Taking advice from others is fine—even desirable—as long as you're taking it from the right people. People who are wise and godly, who know what they're talking about and have an objective opinion to offer. Not people with a hidden (or obvious) agenda (or people who have grandchildren at stake in your decision).

For some women, the answer is simple. Get married, have sex, get pregnant. Then get pregnant again. And again.

For others, the solution isn't so cut-and-dried. Some women want to work on their marriages for a while before they have babies. Some have a career that means a lot to them. Some just don't feel ready to be mothers. Some are ready but can't get pregnant. There's a lot to think about.

Start a family soon after your honeymoon, and you might find yourself wishing you'd had more time to cement your marriage before baby bulldozed onto the scene. (If baby came on the scene before your marriage, you *really* know what I'm talking about.)

Make the decision to wait five or ten years, and you might find the transition to parenthood to be one never-ending bout with what feels like culture shock and jet lag.

There's no right way to start a family. If you and your husband already know (and agree on) your family plan, go with it. If not, spend time in prayer and lots of honest communication.

The Family Plan (Subject to Change)

Where do we come up with the plans we make? How do we decide how many kids we'd like to have and when we'd like to start having them?

A number of things come into play: your personality, your dreams for a career or ministry, and how you feel about the family you grew up in. Of course, throw your husband's ideas into the mix, and you might find this family-planning thing a bit challenging.

I asked some married women without children to share their plans with me. I was interested to see how many kids they wanted and why.

> "Since I'm from a family of eight, I am leaning toward having a larger family, but we'll see how the first one goes."

> "We both came from a family of four kids and aren't sure we want to try to handle that many ourselves. It seems odd that we would only want three when we were both the fourth child in our families, but at this point, we still only want three."

> "I would like four kids. My husband came from a big family and doesn't argue about how many kids I want. He just says we'll see. He's not into planning out his entire future before it even happens like I am."

> "I'd like four to six kids, but he wants two-ish. I came from a family of five kids, and I love having that many siblings."

> "My husband and I are leaving the number of kids completely up to God. We both strongly disagree with birth control, as we believe only God truly knows what's best for us. We're hoping for a bunch of kids."

> "I see myself having three or four kids. My sister and I didn't have any other siblings growing up, and we were lonely. We used to beg our parents to have more kids. At one time my husband said we were going to have thirteen children. Now he says eight."

> "I come from a family of two, so that is a familiar, comfortable number for me. The idea of more than two kids overwhelms me."

"We envision having four kids. We've evolved into this number over time. We both feel God is leading us to adopt internationally, and we'd love to adopt two children so none of our kids is the sole 'different' face in the family pictures. So at least two adopted plus two biological makes at least four!"

"We both want a lot of kids. Eight seems good."

"I've always wanted a large family, but my husband comes from a family of eight kids, so he knows that a big family has drawbacks. My mother-in-law has actually been trying to talk me off the big-family ledge, saying that I will not have a life if I have more than four. We'll probably end up with three. I always go back and forth between a big family and a smaller one because I would like to have a career too."

"I would like to have at least three—biological and/or adopted. My husband would like to have an even number. He was the oldest of three boys and felt like the younger two always ganged up on him."

"We would like to have one or two kids someday. I am an only child, and my husband is the youngest of seven in a blended family. I grew up with countless opportunities he did not. So we agree that we only want two kids tops so that we can always provide them with some of life's pleasures and luxuries."

"We're thinking two or three, but we're going to play it by ear. I think God will let us know how many we should have. If we have three boys, adopting a little girl might be in order. Or if we have little hellions, we might stop at two!"

"I'd like to have three, possibly four kids. I think five (like my parents had) were a bit difficult to handle as we all entered the lovely teen years. I want enough kids so they can enjoy each other and learn to share, but I want to be able to pay attention to each of them (and have enough money that they don't feel destitute). It's hard enough to pay attention to one kid, so maybe we'll go with three. Or two. Or none."

As I mentioned, I originally wanted four kids. We have three and are perfectly content—unless God should lead us to adopt in the future.

When I was pregnant with my first, I remember telling a wise woman that I wanted four kids just like my mom. "Honey," she said kindly, "four kids today isn't what it was in your mama's day."

Whatever, I thought. Glad I didn't say it out loud.

As a general rule, the number of children women say they want before they have kids is equal to or greater than how many they actually have. Much less common is the woman who increases her ideal family size after the fact. Quite often, we love the idea of having tons of kids. The reality of it is a whole new ball game.

I'm no prophet, but I'm generally pretty good at predicting how many children certain women will be able to handle. When they give me a staggering figure, I smile and say, "Sounds great!" Then I sit back and watch.

Big families are awesome—a true blessing from God—but they take a special kind of mama (and daddy!) and an incredible amount of sacrifice. Like it or not, this *isn't* our mama's day. But that's all I'm going to say about that.

Ready...Set...Go!

So when should you start this family of yours? You should probably be ready for kids on your wedding night. I personally believe that using family planning methods is fine, but God reserves the right to bless your womb in spite of them.

Your choice will depend on your circumstances, your finances, your hubby, your goals, how many children you want, and all that.

I have one sweet friend who says she's too selfish right now to have kids. (She is *not* selfish, but generous and kind.) She and her husband have been married for six years, and she thinks "you should wait until you can selflessly give up everything you have to love your child. I think people prematurely get baby envy, have kids, and make lousy parents. Hopefully, I'll feel ready at some point, but currently, I acknowledge that I'm selfish, and I like it just being me and my husband still."

The bad news is this: Selflessly giving up your life for your child will never be easy. In fact, it will probably only get harder as time goes by.

One woman (married five years) seemed to grasp this concept. "Our goal is to have our debt paid off and have a strong marriage before we have children," she says. "However, it seems the longer we are married without kids, the more comfortable and content we become, and the harder it will be to transition to the phase of having children."

Well said. Quite true.

Selflessness just isn't a whole lot of fun any way you look at it. We like ourselves. And we like doing life our own way. Thankfully, in God's economy, giving yourself away is the only thing that brings true fulfillment in the end.

So ask God for His wisdom. When your plan meshes with His, you know for a fact you're on the right route.

But remember, having a plan in place doesn't guarantee it will come to fruition.

The Waiting Game

When I was young, my Sunday school teacher told me that God answers prayers three ways—yes, no, and wait. I can usually handle yes and no. I'm not so good at wait. But God has taught me many things while delaying the fulfillment of my dreams.

I remember a time when I was desperate for a simple yes, but God's answer was a four-letter word—w-a-i-t.

Here are some excerpts from my journal nearly a decade ago:

August: "I wish with all my heart that I were pregnant. I can't remember ever wanting something as much as I want a baby right now. *God, bless my womb and give us a baby!*"

September: "I want a baby. I cannot imagine how incredibly unreal and amazing it will feel when I find out I'm pregnant. Yikes! We want a baby!"

October: "Today's my birthday. Happy birthday to me. It would be a lot happier if I had a little baby growing inside of me. Oh, I want a baby!"

November: "I never completely give up hope until I have at least two negative pregnancy tests. I think God is making me wait so I will appreciate His precious gift even more."

December: "I can't believe this year is almost over. I want so badly to get pregnant!"

January: "This is our sixth month of trying for a baby. I really wish I could get pregnant! I know God's timing is best, but it doesn't make me want a baby any less. I went through a rough time over New Year's. It seems like everyone is pregnant but me."

February: "I'm crying because I want a baby. Seven months is a long time to keep getting your hopes up and then having them dashed to little bits. *God, I know You have many things to teach me through this. I know it will all make sense to me someday. Help me not to miss out on Your blessings because I'm feeling sorry for myself.*"

March: "I want to have a baby so badly. *Lord, please, please, please let me get pregnant this month! I don't know what I'll do if I don't. Well, I know what I'll do. I'll trust You and try, try again. It's just so hard. I want a baby!*"

We started trying in August, and I got pregnant in March. I'm so thankful I kept a record of my thoughts and feelings during those eight months. Looking back, God's hand in my life was so evident.

After I had given birth to my first baby, I had a friend who was trying to get pregnant. After just one month, she gave me a sob story about how depressed she felt, how devastated she was that she didn't get pregnant right away.

I hope the look on my face didn't betray the feelings in my heart at that moment. I felt like smacking her.

"Are you kidding me?" I wanted to scream. "*One month?* Are you for stinking *real?* You tried for *one month,* and you're acting like your life is over? Give me a break!"

And then I realized how small and insignificant my eight-month wait must have seemed to another friend who had been trying for a year and a half without a positive pregnancy test. Or my friend who tried for five years and then adopted. Or my friend who recently learned that her husband is physically unable to father a child. And on and on the list goes.

Looking back, the two times it took me months and months to conceive seem like drops in the bucket. And they were. But at the time, I experienced very real disappointment and pain. And I learned lessons I never would have learned otherwise.

Waiting for a baby was one of the most trying experiences in my life. It nearly consumed me at times. But God knew what He was doing. If patience is a virtue, I was hopelessly un-virtuous.

Eventually, I learned to give complete control of my life over to God. I couldn't do a single thing to make my dreams come true. I had to acknowledge that I was nothing without Him.

Thanks, Hannah!

During those months, God spoke to me through the Bible story of Hannah—a woman who longed for a baby but couldn't get pregnant. I was struck by the number of other big Bible names—Sarah, Rebekah, Rachel, Elizabeth—who were barren for a time before God opened their wombs.

This infertility theme runs throughout the pages of Scripture. God is not a cruel dictator who withholds our desires from us out of spite. He is a loving Father who knows that learning to patiently wait will ultimately strengthen our character and make us more like Him.

I journaled a prayer to God just a couple weeks before I got pregnant, not knowing, of course, that He was just about ready to fill my ever-lovin' uterus with an eensy-teensy babe.

> *Devotions at school yesterday morning were about Hannah crying out to You to bless her womb and give her a baby. I know what she's going through, Lord. (Except that I'm my husband's only wife.)*
>
> *I read her story again today when I woke up. I know—I'm a glutton for punishment. I just love reading about her misery and crying out to You because that's what I'm feeling right now.*
>
> *The hard part is this—her story has a happy ending. I don't know yet if mine will. God, I want to promise You all sorts of things. Like, just give me a baby, and I'll name him Samuel (Samantha if it's a girl) and send him to the temple once he's weaned.*
>
> *It's easy for me to say. It might be harder to actually do. I know one thing—I'm having a hard time giving You my baby right now. I should put this whole baby thing in Your hands and say, "Your will be done, Father."*
>
> *Yet I keep clinging to my dreams. I'm not willing to give them up.*
>
> *God, please help me surrender this to You. I'm hoping once I do, You'll give it all right back to me. But there's always the possibility that You won't. Help me trust that You truly know what's best for me even though I can't imagine that being anything but a baby.*
>
> *I wonder how long Hannah struggled with infertility. It says*

she longed for a child year after year. Give me the strength to wait as long as You need me to.

Me, Myself, and I

TTC (Trying To Conceive) time can turn into such a selfish thing so quickly. It did for me anyway. I became consumed with myself— my body, my cycle, my desires, my disappointment.

Meeting my husband's sexual and emotional needs was difficult. So was being excited for friends and relatives who were getting pregnant. I had a hard time pursuing my relationship with God when He wasn't giving me what I wanted.

Yet God, in His goodness, didn't give up on me.

He showed me ways to unselfishly love my husband instead of just using him for his sperm. (You can read about that in chapter 13 of my book *Is That All He Thinks About?* I do hate to repeat myself!)

God also exposed my jealousy for what it was. Here's another prayer from my journal:

Lord, I looked up the words "jealousy" and "envy" today to see what the difference is between the two.

I am ashamed to admit that I am feeling jealous, which, apparently, is much worse than feeling envious. Envy is where you want something that someone else has. If you both had it, you'd be okay with that. Jealousy says, "I want it, and I don't want you to have it."

Someone I know is pregnant. I don't want her to be pregnant. I want to be pregnant. I happen to know that she wasn't even trying.

I am seething with jealousy. Lord, this emotion inside of me is so alive that it scares me. I can feel it eating away at the inside of my soul. Am I really such a terrible person that I would have such nasty feelings in my heart?

Evidently so.

It's unfair, and I'm angry. I'm the one who should have a baby in my belly, not her!

I don't know how You're going to strip these sinful feelings of jealousy away, but I need You to do it. I can't give it up to You right now. I need You to force it away from me.

You have shown me what a rotten, sinful heart I have. Help me to love this person, Lord. True love does not choose jealousy.

Please give me a second chance.

And God helped me see that life isn't all about me getting what I want. More important things are at stake.

As I looked back on my life, I realized I'd been pretty spoiled. I didn't eat off of silver platters, but kind of.

No, we weren't rich growing up, but I've never lacked for anything. If I needed something, I got it. And if I wanted something bad enough, I did extra chores and saved up money until I could afford it. In school, if I wanted good grades, I got them. If I wanted a boyfriend, I got one.

Then all that changed. I wanted a baby. And I couldn't have it.

Is that the point? I asked the Lord. *Are You trying to show me what life is like when I don't get everything I want? Are You trying to teach me a lesson I could never learn if I was never denied anything?*

The denial hurt, but it was growing me. It built up a layer of perseverance and character in my soul that never existed before. It sliced through that veneer of self-confidence, ripped it to shreds, and put a coating of God-reliance in its place.

I was a better person for the waiting.

Keep the Eraser Handy

I remember being in high school and wanting things in my life to work out in a certain way. I clung to Proverbs 16:3: "Commit to the LORD whatever you do, and your plans will succeed."

I had my plans all laid out. I simply told God, *I commit this to*

You, and expected Him to honor part B of the verse—"your plans will succeed."

My theology was obviously a bit skewed. Committing something to the Lord is somewhat more complicated than stating what you want and tacking a Bible phrase at the end of it for good measure.

In retrospect, I'm so glad I didn't actually get some of the things I asked God for and "committed" to Him.

Funny how I skimmed right over some of the verses around Proverbs 16:3. Like verse 1—"To man belong the plans of the heart, but from the LORD comes the reply of the tongue."

And verse 9—"In his heart a man plans his course, but the LORD determines his steps."

Planning your life is a noble thing as long as you do it in pencil and not with a Sharpie. And get the biggest pink eraser you can find, hand it to God, and say, "You reserve the right to change this plan however You see fit. And I promise not to throw fits when eraser shavings start falling all over the place."

Could It Be?

On a lighter note, in all those months of trying to get pregnant, I became the queen of imaginary symptoms. I read too much, plain and simple. I had chapter 1 of *The Girlfriend's Guide to Pregnancy* practically memorized before I even got knocked up.

Every month—same. I micro-analyzed every single thing that happened in my body from ovulation to when my period was supposed to start. I tried my hardest to make each bodily function or reaction fit into my list of early pregnancy symptoms.

Something would smell funny in the fridge. Sensitivity to odors is a pregnancy symptom. Maybe I'm pregnant! (Or it could be the onions on the leftover pizza.)

I'd feel really drowsy in the middle of the day. I just wanted to take a nap. Fatigue—another pregnancy symptom! (Of course, I went to bed at 2:00 a.m. the past two nights and started my day as a teacher a mere four hours later. That might explain the tiredness.)

I'd been peeing a lot lately. Frequent urination! Pregnant women pee constantly! (Yeah, and so do women who have been drinking 64 ounces of water a day to clear up their skin. So much for that.)

I'd feel a little crampy. Phantom menstrual cramps—another symptom! (Of course, they could be *real* menstrual cramps. Yep, that's what they are.)

Why couldn't I just take a hint? Not pregnant! Not pregnant! Not pregnant! Most of those symptoms weren't going to come until after I'd missed a period anyway. And I hadn't missed any!

Who was I kidding? I was only driving myself insane!

And Then...

And then it happened. I got pregnant. Pregnant!

My last period had started at the beginning of March. We were preparing to make a move for Gabe's job and were scoping out apartments in our new town. According to my brilliant calculations, we would be in a hotel room during the best two days to try. How perfect!

Except that Gabe was sick the first night and had dislocated his shoulder the next. No cigar. (No sex either.)

Our last week in our old apartment was filled with late nights of packing and not much sex. (Okay, none.)

On our first night in our new apartment (much, much too late in my cycle to make a baby, according to my ingenious estimations), we celebrated our move with some lovin'. And let me tell you, it was the first time in a long time we had made love just for the heck of it. It was quite a night.

I expected to start my period April fourth or fifth. When I didn't, I took a test on the seventh. It was negative. I was bummed, but not surprised. You can't expect to get pregnant if you don't have sex when you're ovulating, eh? And I had been sick for a week with the flu and a sinus infection. That would explain the delay in my period.

So on April 11, I'd been well for four days and still hadn't started. At first, I was just mad. "I wish I would start already! How am I going to know when I can try again if I don't start my period?"

Then the unthinkable occurred to me. What if I had miscalculated my cycle (no!) and taken the test too soon? What if I took another test, just in case?

I talked to Gabe and he suggested waiting at least two days so I wouldn't waste a test. This hobby of mine was getting expensive.

I agreed to wait. Then as soon as he left for work that morning, I went (peed on a stick) behind his back.

Three minutes later, I took a peek. Negative. Just like all the others. Disappointed again. I literally had the test in my hand, suspended over the trash can, milliseconds away from letting it drop, when...wait! The light bounced off the test window at just the right angle, and I noticed what looked like a really faint line. My overeager eyes were just playing tricks, right?

I brought it close to my face (gross, I know). There was a *line*. A faint, faint, faint line. And the directions said that even if the line is really light, you're probably pregnant. I just stared and stared at that line, wondering if I was imagining it. And somehow, it seemed to be getting darker.

It was definitely there. A line! But, the directions also said that if you wait too long to read the test, something that *looks* like a line could start to appear. Aaaahhh!!!

I ended up taking three pregnancy tests. All of them showed a line, but each line was really faint. So I looked up a doctor in the phone book and scheduled an appointment. She gave me a urine test and told me it was positive, "but the line is very faint" (ya think?), so she wanted me to have a blood test too.

The lab technician told me the blood test results would take two days. Are you kidding me? But the kind lady at the checkout counter told me in hushed tones that I'd probably know by the following day.

At 9:40 the next morning, I got a phone call.

"May I speak to Marla Taviano?"

"That's me."

"Well, we have the results of your bloodwork."

"And...?"

"And you are."

Breathe. Breathe. "I'm what?"

"You're pregnant."

"I'm pregnant?"

"You're pregnant!"

"Woooohoooo! Thank you so much!"

I dropped to my knees, thanked the Lord, called Gabe at work, and jumped around the house like a lunatic until I collapsed on the couch in exhaustion.

Sharing the Happy News

I know lots of people wait at least three months before they share their news. I honestly don't know how they do it. Notoriously bad secret keepers, Gabe and I didn't have a prayer. We waited all of three days.

We were heading to Gabe's parents' house for the weekend. His grandparents were celebrating their fiftieth anniversary. Our plan was to tell his parents Friday night and the rest of his family on Saturday. We'd tell my parents at the anniversary party on Sunday.

Our Friday night plan was ingenious. Rock (Gabe's dad) had hooked up our washer and dryer for us when we moved into our new apartment three weeks before. He had been concerned that it might leak. It hadn't, but we worked it into our plan.

Gabe and I loaded up a garbage bag of "dirty laundry," which actually consisted of clean towels, socks, and baby clothes. When Rock got home from work at 11:30 p.m., we would bring in the clothes, look all frustrated, and say, "Can we do our laundry here? Our washer is leaking all over the place."

Gabe would begin "sorting" the laundry, they'd see the baby clothes, and…you get the picture.

Well, we were still visiting at Gabe's grandma's house when his dad got off work. As we sat talking in the living room, Rock asked me, "So, how is your washer working? Has it leaked at all?"

Oh dear. This was not part of the plan! I rolled my eyes and shrugged. "We'll talk about it later," I said.

"What happened?" Rock asked, concerned. "It's leaking, isn't it?"

"We can talk about it when we get home," I said. "Don't worry about it."

We left for Gabe's parents' house soon afterward. In the car, I told Gabe about my conversation with his dad. We laughed.

We pulled in, and Gabe lugged in the bag of laundry. "Is it okay if we do some laundry here?" he asked. He started pulling clothes out of the bag.

"Don't you guys have a washer?" his brother asked.

His mom pulled me into the laundry room and wanted me to show her exactly what had gone wrong. I didn't want to miss Gabe pulling out the baby clothes, so I made up something about some hose or pipe and rushed back out to Gabe and Rock.

Gabe was holding up a onesie. My stomach was full of butter-flies. "Why are you washing these *now?*" Gabe asked me, according to plan.

"Because I didn't want to wait until December," I replied.

No one got it. They all just stood there.

Finally, Gabe's brother asked, "Are you *pregnant?*"

"No," Gabe's dad said.

I smiled.

"*Are* you?" his dad asked as his mom ran out from the laundry room.

We nodded. Everybody hugged. And brushed away happy tears.

We couldn't wait to tell the rest of Gabe's family. The following evening, we were all sitting around the living room at his grandparents' house eating ice cream. Talk had turned to our upcoming family vacation in North Carolina that summer.

Gabe cleared his throat and asked for everyone's attention. "We have a question for all of you," he began. "Would it be okay if we brought a guest to Ocean Isle this summer?"

I enjoyed watching the strange and puzzled looks all around the room. No one seemed too thrilled with the idea, but I could tell no one wanted to say anything.

"We thought there would be room with Lori and Jenny," Gabe said. Lori and Jenny were sisters who would be sharing a room in our condo.

Gabe's grandma piped up, "If you want to bring a friend, he can sleep in *your* bed!" She pointed at Gabe and me.

I stood up and put my hands on my belly. "Don't worry," I said, smiling. "We'll keep her right in here the whole time."

More hearty congrats and hugs.

The next day was the big fiftieth bash. I was getting nervous waiting for my parents to arrive. If my plan was going to work, it was imperative that I catch them before they came inside. Gabe came out too. And his dad, who wanted to watch the action from behind some bushes like a little kid.

When they pulled up to the hotel, I ran out to their car and motioned for them to park next to ours. They were prepared for this. I had told them a few days before that I had a box of things to return to them.

Mom and Dad got out of their car, we hugged, and Gabe brought over the box. I began pulling items out one by one to "make sure everything is really yours."

"Is this Bethany's jacket?" Check. "Is this Dad's video on Japan?" Check. "Is this...Is this...Is this...?" Check. Check. And check.

Then I pulled out a kids' book and read the title, "I'm Glad I'm Your Grandpa."

"Never seen it before," my mom said.

I tried not to laugh, as I turned to Dad. "I'm glad I'm your *grandpa?*" I repeat. "You're not a grandpa. You won't be a grandpa until *December*."

After a second or two, it sunk in. Mom squealed. Dad beamed. Everybody hugged. Rock climbed out of the bushes and joined in.

Tears came to my eyes as I silently thanked God for His bountiful blessings. The next eight months were going to be full of love and excitement.

2

From Womb to World

Pregnancy, like no other time in your life, is a roller coaster in every sense of the word. From the nausea to the up-and-down thoughts, fears, and emotions, it's easy to feel utterly overwhelmed.

You start thinking about things that have never crossed your mind before. You start worrying about things that have always seemed under control. You start regretting things you've done or haven't done, relationships that aren't what they could be.

At first, nothing seems real. You're beside yourself with elation, bursting at the seams, just waiting to fall off of cloud nine. But it still doesn't seem like reality.

Slowly but surely, nausea sets in. You pray you'll be able to handle morning sickness with grace. Maybe the thought of throwing up horrifies you. You so want to be a good pregnant woman. You don't want to complain all the time. You don't want to get moody. You don't want to be self-centered. You don't want to have raging hormones. Is it possible to avoid all those things?

You're so excited to do all the things that mommies do—cuddle your baby, nurse her, fold his little clothes, change her diaper, wash him in that little bathtub, listen to him giggle and coo, watch her daddy interact with her.

And you so want to teach this little baby about God—to teach him how to pray, to read her Bible stories, to explore creation together, to instill biblical morals and values in his little heart.

Oh, the thought of all that just thrills your soul—and wears you out! You're so tired lately. So, so tired. If you can just make it through the rest of the afternoon…It's amazing how much extra energy it takes to grow a baby!

You track the growth of your baby every single week. He's the size of a grain of rice. Then a pea. Then a raisin. Then an inch long. Then two, three, four, twelve inches! Your clothes get snug. Your pregnancy books say your uterus just keeps doubling in size.

You worry when you measure small or gain too much or have any kind of cramping. You're afraid to eat, drink, or ingest anything that might harm your baby in any way. Your husband is afraid that sex will hurt the baby. He's so overprotective he thinks that laughing too hard will shake the baby's brain.

Everyone you meet has some words of wisdom to share. Your face is pudgy—it's a girl. You're carrying low—it's a boy. You look like a watermelon—it's a girl.

Strangers want to talk to you and pet you and elicit deeply personal information from you. Sometimes you eat up the attention. Other times you wish you had some pepper spray.

You don't recognize your body. Strange, strange things are happening to it all the time. You're having vivid, graphic dreams about childbirth—dreams not suitable for print. Feeling the baby move is a sensation you wish you could bottle up and save forever. Even when that little bugger kicks you in the ribs so hard you gasp.

You don't know how it happened, but you know you're a different person than you were before this little one came to occupy your womb. And you're starting to realize you will never, ever be the same again.

And that's okay. You're ready to be a mommy.

The Good, the Bad, and the Ugly

Tons of great books on pregnancy are available. I pored over them constantly with each of my babies. I couldn't get enough of what my baby looked like and what she was doing each and every miraculous day.

I'll leave the physical and medical details to the pregnancy experts. I'll address some of that stuff, sure. Who doesn't like a little gory exchange of pregnancy and childbirth details? (Oh, you *don't?*) But I'll mostly be dealing with the emotional and spiritual issues we preggo women face.

I'm always intrigued to hear what women like and dislike about being pregnant. We share so much in common, yes, but no two pregnancies are identical.

You'll have women who barely survive the nine months, puking their guts out, in and out of the hospital and on bed rest. Then there are those who morph into goddesses the moment their child is conceived, glowing and grinning and thriving for nine glorious months. Most of us fall somewhere in between.

I asked women to tell me which parts of pregnancy were their favorites and which parts they could have happily done without. We'll start with the happy.

> "The ultrasounds. Seeing that little baby all squeezed in there, moving around or just chilling out."

> "Feeling the baby move, getting all that attention and a whole new wardrobe, being free from periods for nine whole months."

> "Seeing my husband's face when he heard the baby's heartbeat. The race to try to get him to feel the baby move, only to have it stop as soon as his hand touched my belly."

> "It's the only time my stomach is truly tight—without crunches!"

> "Trying to identify body parts as they moved along my belly."

> "When it was over!"

"My husband telling me how beautiful I looked and how much he loved our 'belly bean.' He was always rubbing my stomach."

"Eating, eating, eating, eating!"

"Feeling my precious little ones rolling around in my womb."

"Consuming Arby's on a regular basis and assuring myself it was all for the health of my child."

"Bigger boobs!"

"Feeling confident and beautiful (hot!), turning heads for the first time in my life. That pregnancy glow. Not caring about my pant size or 'sucking it in.' "

"I loved the butterflies when the baby kicked—something only I could fully feel and understand."

"Feeling like part of a special club and hearing all the questions people would ask."

"The second trimester. The sickness faded, I had more energy, people could tell I was pregnant, and I wasn't feeling like a beached whale...yet."

"I loved feeling like I was the only person who had ever been pregnant."

"The hospital stay, where I was waited on hand and foot. I was deathly ill for nine straight months, so that's the only part I loved!"

And what was the worst part of those nine loooong months?

"Ugh. Throwing up over and over, the pelvic pain, watching my body get gross-looking, not being able to sleep at night..."

"My ankles and calves swelling two times bigger and only being able to wear my husband's flip-flops."

"The constant spitting in the sink, the sciatic pain when walking, and the overall feeling of being fat and ugly."

"Terrible morning (all-day) sickness. Throwing up in my hand as I tried to pull my car over on the way to work. A commercial for Denny's omelets on the radio set my stomach over the edge before I knew it."

"Being five feet tall and carrying twins. I couldn't drive the last month or so because I had to move the seat back so far, I couldn't reach the pedals!"

"Breathing became a chore!"

"I felt spiritually out of whack. I would open my Bible and just stare at it. I felt so overwhelmed."

"The heightened sense of smell. I moved the hamper out of the house and took the garbage disposal apart twice!"

"An awful metallic aftertaste that lasted the entire pregnancy."

"Sex was uncomfortable and awkward. I never had the typical increased desire for sex in the second trimester."

"People saying hurtful things about my weight."

"Sleeping upright in the La-Z-Boy for a good part of my pregnancy."

"I had the worst migraines of my life. I was hormonal and felt obsessive-compulsive about stupid things, like how the sheets should be folded."

"Being enormous, working really hard even though all I wanted to do was sleep, being enormous, listening to people say, 'You're almost ready to pop!' when I still had eight weeks left, and being enormous."

A Very Real Fear

Most of us deal with fear in some way during our pregnancy. Fear of the unknown. Fear of miscarriage. Fear of something being wrong with our baby when he's born.

When I was pregnant for the first time, I had some spotting and a tiny bit of cramping early on. After all I had read, I was convinced it was an ectopic pregnancy. I bawled my eyes dry for two days, crying out to God to save my baby.

I called my doctor, and she told me to come in for a checkup. I wrote this letter to my unborn baby when I got home:

> Dear Little One,
>
> I had an ultrasound today and watched your tiny heart beat! I saw your tiny perfect body! Praise the Lord!
>
> Baby, I cried and cried and prayed and prayed that God would protect you and keep you whole and safe. I am so incredibly grateful to Him! I can hardly contain myself!
>
> I am six weeks pregnant, and already your little heart is beating beautifully. After my ultrasound, the doctor left so I could change back into my clothes, and I got down on my knees and thanked Jesus. He has been so good to us, baby. I want to spend the rest of my life showing you just how wonderful our God is.
>
> And more than anything else, I want you to give your life to Him. Besides the day you were born, that day will be the happiest day of your life for me.
>
> > I love you, sweet baby!
> > Mommy

A Baby Waiting in Heaven

That baby is almost seven now, but four years later, my third pregnancy did end in a miscarriage. I won't spend tons of time talking about it, but should you need these words of encouragement someday, they'll be here.

After almost a year of trying for baby number three, I got pregnant.

A week after my positive test, I began bleeding and lost the baby. Yes, I was devastated, but by God's grace, it was one of the least traumatic miscarriages a woman could have.

I'd just like to share a few snippets of my journal during that time to show you God's faithfulness and goodness.

Lord, I can't really see through my tears. This is so hard. I've been bleeding for about three hours now. I'm about 80 percent sure I'm miscarrying. God, I know You're a miracle worker and can still save my baby. But I also know that You give and take away. And I know You love me and will get me through this.

I went to bed at 10:00 last night but couldn't go to sleep for at least an hour. At one point, I started bawling and came downstairs and asked Gabe to hold me. At 2:00, I woke up with the worst headache of my life.

I lost the baby. The worst may be over. As Gabe was leaving a little bit ago, he leaned down and talked to Livi and Ava. Little Ava looked at him and said, "I'm not a big sister any more." Break my heart. I lost it.

Heal my heart, God. Help me to be strong for my girls. They hate seeing Mommy hurting.

Lord, I don't understand this, but I really do trust You. I know You're growing me—making me better able to understand the pain of others. Thank You for trusting me with a miscarriage. I feel honored that You thought I could handle it with grace. It hurts, God—physically, but mostly emotionally. Please don't ever make me go through one again.

Lord, losing a baby is hard. I know now just how badly I wanted one. Give us another baby soon!

Gabe spent the day at the radio station. Four women came up to him and said they were praying for me—they'd all had miscarriages. One woman had five! I feel like I've been hit by a truck. I'm really crampy and bleeding and my head hurts.

At bedtime last night, Ava said, "I know who made the baby die. I did. I made the baby die." I felt my heart rip.

"No, you didn't, sweetie. Nobody made the baby die."

"Uh-huh. I was talking and talking, and I made the baby die. Daddy said be quiet, and I didn't."

Rip, rip, rip goes my heart. I tried so hard to comfort her.

After I put her to bed, she started bawling, "I miss my baby sister! I want my baby sister to come back!"

I just rocked her and cried with her.

I feel good, Lord—mentally and physically. I know it's the prayers of Your people. I can feel them. I wish it wouldn't have happened, but thank You for making it as painless as a miscarriage can be.

I feel a little sad right now—and empty. My head hurts, and I feel a little crampy. I think I'm trying to rush this whole recovery thing just a bit.

The Sun Shines Again

Without giving TMI, just let me say that I know exactly which day I got pregnant again. Looking back on my journal entry that day (just hours before Nina was conceived) proves to me that God used my miscarriage to make me more like Christ. Praise His name!

The days are flying, yet it seems like forever ago when we lost our baby, just a little over a month ago. I remember when it happened I was so tempted to just survive, counting the days until I got pregnant again. But then God filled me with His joy, and I realized what a huge blessing each day really is.

Now I'm enjoying my husband, our girls, my writing,

preparing for speaking engagements. I'm enjoying the weather, the sunshine, the leaves popping out on the trees, the dandelions.

I woke up this morning with the greatest feeling. The window was open, the breeze was tantalizing, the birds twirping. I praised the Lord for a while, realizing sadly that I do that so rarely. I usually just jump in, surrender my day to Him (when I remember), and start rattling off my list.

Forgive me, Lord, for neglecting to praise You.

I am beautifully overwhelmed.

A year earlier, when we first started trying for that baby, Gabe and I were playing a friendly game of Scrabble and made a bet. If I won the game, our baby would be a girl. If Gabe won, it would be a boy.

I kept pulling further and further ahead, but near the end of the game, Gabe made a huge almost-comeback by using all his letters to spell the word "journey."

I still won by 37. It's a girl!

Then I suddenly remembered something and checked the rule book. Sure enough, if you use all seven letters in one turn, a 50-point bonus for you!

Gabe won by 13. It's a boy!

Ten loooong months later came my pregnancy and miscarriage. Poor little Ava cried herself to sleep every night for a month. It was always the same—"I miss my baby sister!"

I don't believe that every little thing in life is a sign from God, but I took that as a sign—that itty-bitty baby we lost was a girl.

Then one day I remembered that fateful Scrabble game—I had kept the score sheet. A thought occurred to me, and my tummy twisted into a knot.

I will probably never have a son—except for the young men my girls marry in a few (30) years. But what if I get to heaven one day and see a curly-headed little boy running toward me, arms outstretched, enveloping me in a tackle-hug, and crying, "Mama!"

Wouldn't that be just like God?

Ready or Not

Oh, what a wild, emotional ride, this thing called pregnancy! By the time the days on your pregnancy ticker have dwindled down to single digits, one crazy emotion begins to trump them all—the realization that what goes in must come out.

Over these last nine months, your baby has been developing and growing. And growing and growing. Just like one of those ships in a bottle, assembled piece by piece. Then the mast is pulled up, and *voila!*

Somehow, some way, this baby is going to want to make an entrance into this world. And being the educated woman you are, you know it can only happen one of two ways. Slicing you open with a knife or *huge ship coming out of tiny mouth of bottle*. Frankly, neither appeal to you.

I'm not sure why we get so worked up over this labor and delivery stuff. What's the big deal? It's not like a bazillion other women haven't already done this before.

You do realize, don't you, that there are gals all over the world right this very moment, squatting in rice fields, stopping their work long enough to pop a baby out, cutting the cord with a machete, strapping the tiny things to their chests, and getting on with life?

Ha! Just having a little fun with you, that's all.

Giving birth is a big deal. Huge. And regardless of how many grillion women have done it, you'll feel like you're a virtual pioneer!

Just like conception and every little bit of your baby's in-womb development, childbirth is a complete and utter miracle. I still have no idea how your body knows when the baby is ready to come out and acts accordingly. It's bizarre.

And I *really* have no idea how something so huge fits through an opening so small. (And if you've heard it's like pooping a watermelon, relax! Think more like a smallish cantaloupe.)

The not-knowing-what-to-expect factor might be the worst part of all. Most of us haven't experienced a lot of physical pain up to this point. Sure, you've had a cavity or two. You skinned your knee a few times as a kid. Maybe you've even suffered from migraines or broken your wrist. But you're thinking this just might be pain on a whole new level.

You just might be right. And it's perfectly okay to be a little apprehensive.

Verses to Comfort You

Every other year or so, I like to read through the Bible in its entirety. I'm always amazed at the things that jump out at me. Same words, different point in my life. That's the wonder of God's Word—it's more than a book; it's alive and active.

I was pregnant most of the year 2000 with our first baby. And as I read through the Bible, I again saw it with new eyes—mommy eyes. Every verse about babies and children and mothers and fathers was especially dear to my heart.

If you're looking for verses to bring comfort to your soul as you prepare to give birth, there are a plethora of them. Just do yourself a favor and look in Psalms.

Big and pregnant, I stumbled across a verse in Isaiah about childbirth and did something very foolish—I checked the concordance to find others on the topic. Bad idea.

If you haven't yet given birth, go grab your Bible and some paper clips. Open to the books of Isaiah and Jeremiah—without reading any of the words—and paper-clip them shut! Do not even allow yourself to *accidentally* open your Bible to anything written by these two men until you have safely delivered your darling babe.

You didn't know there were verses in the Bible about labor and childbirth, did you? Oh, yes. Anytime a Bible author wanted to describe something gravely painful or intensely horrific, he would refer to a woman in labor.

Toward the end of my pregnancy, I couldn't even read these verses without cringing.

Isaiah talks about gasping and panting (doesn't sound too bad, right?) and how a woman about to give birth "writhes and cries out in her pain" (okay, a little worse).

Jeremiah writes of groans and cries and asks, "Will not pain grip you like that of a woman in labor?" He talks about feebleness and panic and anguish too.

I had to laugh at Jeremiah 30:6, "Can a man bear children? Then why do I see every strong man with his hands on his stomach like a woman in labor, every face turned deathly pale?" I'm picturing my poor, strong hubby with his hands on his belly, his face ashen.

My concordance listed several more verses, but I quit looking them up. These were about all I could stomach.

In the beginning, Eve screwed up, and God told her, "I will greatly increase your pains in childbearing." And to think that if she would have just obeyed God in the Garden, childbirth would be a walk in the park!

Part of me wanted to go natural all the way, to give birth like women of old, like God originally intended. But then I thought, technically, God's actual Plan A was for childbirth to be painless. That's no longer an option, so maybe I should just go with the epidural.

After all, I'd heard some horror stories! You know, there really should be a law against sharing tales of labors gone bad with childbirth virgins!

In a Perfect World

Just for kicks, I asked some of my not-yet-mom friends to share their vision of the ideal childbirth experience. One of the crazy things about birthing babies is how each experience is so different.

Some labors are picture-perfect. Others are hell on earth. Some follow the birth plans to the letter. Some births have nothing in common with the plan except for the final outcome—a baby.

Here are some dreams my friends have for their future labor and delivery experience. Some are completely serious, others a bit tongue-in-cheek. I look forward to their first babies' birthdays, when we can compare their aspirations with their actuality.

"How do you envision your ideal childbirth experience?" I wanted to know. A few gals summed it up quite succinctly.

"Fast."

"Short!"

"Painless."

"EPIDURAL."

"Um…adoption?"

Some aren't quite ready to deal with thoughts of labor at this point.

"I prefer not to envision the childbirth experience, to be honest. I want my husband to be with me. I want to be in the hospital, have an epidural, and have a nice quick delivery. Isn't that what everyone wants?"

"I try not to think about it. I want eight kids, but I don't want to think about the pain."

"Um, I don't really envision my future childbirth experiences as ideal. I imagine them as horrible and scary and stressful and miserable, hoping that if I prepare myself for the worst it won't be quite as shocking. But that's just me."

"I don't know much about labor. I'll read books when the time comes."

"Whoa! Haven't gotten that far. I'm pretty sure it involves an epidural though."

And some have it all planned out…

"I dream of giving birth either at home or at a birthing center with a midwife, following the principles that I learned in the book *Supernatural Childbirth*. My husband and the midwife will be there. I will feel a lot more comfortable in one of those settings than at a hospital. After the baby is born, we will celebrate with our parents and other family members and then enjoy our time alone together as a new family at our home."

"In a hospital, with my husband and trusted doctor. I would like drugs, please. Lord willing, the labor will not go on for too many hours. I can hear you laughing, Marla."

"My hubby in the room with me. Family waiting nearby. A nurse that isn't too involved but is kind and excited. No emergencies. I'd like to do it at least once without an epidural, just to see what women have had to deal with for thousands of years (my friends with children say I will change my mind about this!)."

And here's my personal favorite, from my cousin Kelly, whose tongue (just so you know) is very nearly always lodged in her cheek.

"I start having contractions and go to the hospital five minutes later, where my water immediately breaks. A nurse tells me I am six or seven centimeters already, someone gives me a lovely epidural, and I effortlessly shove the child out, feeling only a bit of pressure. Wait—is seven centimeters too late for an epidural? Or we could schedule a C-section, eliminating labor altogether. (Although I had laparoscopic surgery once, and I had a really tough time after, so I'm not sure how I'd handle a baby and being sliced at the same time.) I hope to avoid a lot of pain through a lot of drugs either way."

Expectations

Several moms mentioned that preconceived ideas and expectations threw them for a serious loop.

"I felt like a failure for needing an emergency C-section with my first baby," says my friend Suzanne. "Of course, it wasn't my fault, but I expected to have a vaginal delivery like my mom had done—six times! She even pushed the sixth baby out breech!"

"I had a totally normal pregnancy," my friend Beki told me, "so during childbirth class, my husband and I goofed off when it was time to talk about C-sections. When my labor wasn't progressing and the nurse told me it was a possibility, I was by myself in the room and began crying so hard. My sister came in and prayed with me. That was the sweetest prayer ever. It was the only time I've ever felt God immediately calm me."

My friend Jessica B. had an intense labor with her daughter—no epidural, just lots of work and excruciating pain. "But seeing her for the first time was such a high," Jess says. "I realized then that birthing children could definitely become an addictive experience."

She was expecting that same high with baby number two, but the epidural changed things. "I was disappointed that the same high wasn't there. I didn't feel like I had worked as hard for him, I guess, so there wasn't that feeling of amazing relief. However, I enjoyed the entire laboring process so much. Instead of wanting to die, I was able to ponder his impending birth and actually laugh the entire time!"

"I think in childbirth—just like in parenting—it is good to not have expectations, or at least keep them realistic," says my friend Anne Marie. "My first birthing experience included an early induction, Pitocin, epidural, Nubane. I was so drugged and frustrated because I felt like I missed everything. I threw up and was shaking and didn't go to the bathroom for two weeks! I couldn't believe the pain I felt for weeks afterward that *no one* told me about! I felt like a failure because of all of the intervention I received. I wish I wouldn't have had preconceived ideas and just been looking forward to the healthy baby!"

The Bestest Day

I always tell people that the day my middle daughter was born was the best day of my life. I know, it sounds like favoritism.

Okay, so I have *four* very special days (one wedding, three births) on the calendar of my memories, but I'm sticking with my story. The day little Ava was born was the most romantic, serene, peaceful day of my life.

Weddings are romantic, yes. And I was thrilled to be marrying Gabe. But wedding days are also stressful. Lots of nerves, so many things that need to come together.

Then you have florists who forget the basket of petals you promised your three-year-old flower girl she would get to carry down the aisle (she carried a leftover boutonniere, and I pitched a small fit over it, but I digress).

The church's reception hall held roughly one-fourth of my guests. I didn't do RSVPs, and more than 500 people showed. Nothing else to do on January 3, I guess. Lots of hugging, smiling, uncomfortable dress. Fabulous, sure, but not serene.

What about the first time I gave birth? Well, my water broke (trickled actually) in the middle of the night, three weeks before my due date. I went to the hospital, less than a centimeter dilated, and started on Pitocin to get my labor going. Thought I would *die* before I got to four centimeters and got the epidural. There's definitely something special about the moment your first child enters the world, but the day wasn't exactly peaceful.

And my youngest daughter's birthday? Thought I was in labor for 12 days before I actually was. Got to hospital. Had her two hours later. Pretty proud of myself for doing the voluntary natural childbirth thing for the first—and last—time. I'll share the whole story in just a bit, but no, it is not romantic and serene to push a nine-plus pound baby out without drugs.

But the day Ava was born? Sigh. I went into labor the night before. Timed contractions. I was up all night with a feverish toddler. I took an early morning shower, put on makeup, made my hair look nice, made arrangements for people to watch Livi at the hospital, and went to my scheduled doctor's appointment. Found out I was already five centimeters dilated.

Got to the hospital—laughing, talking with Gabe, having a marvelous time. Wasn't going to get an epidural, couldn't believe how mild my contractions were. Gabe voted for the epidural. He said he didn't want to watch the baby come out knowing I could feel it. Whatever. But it *was* lovely not feeling a stitch of pain. Everything just worked out so smoothly and perfectly, like a movie script.

That Stand-Out Moment

I asked women to share the most memorable moment of their birthing experiences. Some are sweet, some funny, some just plain crazy—all of them are worth remembering.

"Having my water break just after my husband said, 'You're so dramatic. I never know how much pain you are in.'"

"I was having a C-section, and my daughter was up very high. I remember, in the midst of the surgery, the doctor saying, 'I can't find her,' meaning the baby! He was in up to his shoulder and couldn't figure out where the baby was! I remember saying to my husband, 'Well, I KNOW she's in there!'"

"I remember being so shocked both times at how gooey they were when they came out. Maybe my girls were gooier than most, but I remember being so horrified at the sight of my second daughter that I was totally distracted from the pain of delivering her."

"I'm pushing out this huge baby with no pain medication, and it HURTS. I yell, and my wonderful husband says, 'Oh, come on. This is cool. Push harder!' I'm sure it was sweet and full of daddy pride, but at the moment, I wasn't thinking pleasant thoughts."

"When they handed me my baby, all covered in slimy white cheese."

"Hearing my mom say, 'Do you see that?' to my husband while I'm pushing like mad. I totally freak out, wondering what's wrong. Turns out my daughter has jet black hair at least an inch long. Of course, my husband was a bleached blond at the time, and I'm a redhead! (Her black hair later turned blond—she's definitely his!)"

"My first time in a Jacuzzi! (Although I would rather it had been under different circumstances.)"

"The 45-minute drive to the hospital. Of course, I waited until the last minute to go. Then my husband wanted to stop on the way and buy cigarettes! My mother-in-law (in the backseat) shrieked for him to keep driving. Our son was born 30 minutes after we arrived at the hospital."

"Squeezing my husband's hand so hard I left fingernail marks."

"When I knew I was ready to push and the nurses didn't believe me. When I finally asked them to please check, they clamped my legs together (told my husband to hold them shut!) and went yelling down the hall for my doctor."

"My anesthesiologist. I will love him until the day I die."

"My daughter was born early, so they whisked her away after she came out. Twenty minutes later, they brought her back all clean. She was so beautiful. When my son was born, they immediately plopped him up onto my stomach. He looked so gross and ugly. I was horrified. The doctor must have noticed my reaction because he commented on my 'beautiful son.' After what seemed like forever (probably two minutes), they took him away and cleaned him up. And then I thought he was beautiful."

"I breathed a sigh of relief when my son cried. But I breathed a bigger sigh of relief when my husband, mom, and sister assured me that he was indeed cute."

"After eleven hours of labor and a nonfunctioning epidural, I completely lost my mind. The doctor, who is a family friend, came in and pulled up a chair to chat with my mom.

I was miserable, and from out of nowhere in this growling voice, I shouted, 'There is no talking!' I apologized at my six-week appointment for my violent outburst."

"When I had my second baby at home and my two-year-old daughter climbed up in our bed to meet her baby sister, held her, and without any prompting, began singing 'Jesus Loves Me.' I cried and cried."

Better Her than Me

Some women shared some experiences that I definitely can *not* relate to—thank goodness! Get a load of some of these…

"My mom, an RN, was present for my son's birth," says my friend Terri. "BIG mistake. She took over the labor room, bossed the nurses, and checked my dilation. She even rummaged around in the drawers, produced a fetuscope, put it on her head, and started listening to my belly! I called my husband in, grabbed him by the throat, and shrieked that he had to get rid of my mother. Luckily, my mother-in-law was also there, so she took Mom to a coffee shop. Finally—peace."

"After eight hours of intense, induced labor and no progress, I was wheeled into the operating room for a C-section," Sandi F. says. "I was really tired, goofy from the pain meds, and it was *freezing* in that room. I was dizzy enough to count about 30 people in there! Personnel started to take off my hospital gown to sterile-drape me, and the enormous (300-plus pound) man who started to tie that drape around my neck had the biggest, warmest hands…I just threw my arms all the way around him, hugged him hard, and cried, 'I'm so sorry! I'm sooo cold!' My attempt to warm myself by getting cozy with this stranger required a fresh sterile drape. Most embarrassing moment of my life!"

And you almost have to know Jessica C. to completely appreciate this story…

I had an amazing epidural, so I had a very hard time pushing with feeling. And I couldn't really get the breathing thing down.

"How did I do on that contraction?" I asked my doctor. "Am I doing it right?"

"Not on that one," she said, smiling. "I think you blew it out."

"What?" I said in disbelief. "I poopied?"

The doctor looked at me puzzled. "Um, no...what? I said you blew it out."

"Oh, I'm sorry!" I couldn't believe this was happening. "Really? I poopied?"

She was still puzzled.

"I was so determined not to poopy on the delivery table! That's why I took a water enema at home before we left for the hospital! I didn't want to poopy on the delivery table!"

Somehow, I finally made her understand what I meant. In my mind, "blew it out" meant a blow-out. And a blow-out was what happened when a baby had a poop explosion in his diaper.

"No, I meant you blew out your air before you pushed through the contraction!" She couldn't even stop laughing to help me through my next one.

The entire room was laughing hysterically at me.

Indulge Me

Have you heard Simon Cowell tell American Idol contestants that they're being too indulgent? He usually says it when they stray too far from the standard performance and dare to do something that makes them happy. Like Chris Daughtry singing crazy loud rock or Mandisa belting out some gospel.

According to the dictionary, to indulge is to yield to one's whims and desires, to allow oneself unrestrained gratification. To do something just because you want to.

Sharing my third daughter's birth story at this juncture would definitely qualify as indulgent. Telling my little tale just because I can.

This is straight from my journal the day after her birth nearly two years ago...

> Unbelievable. I couldn't have written a more perfect birth script for Miss Nina Gabriel.
>
> 8:00 a.m.—I start timing contractions off and on. I tell Gabe that this will be Nina's birthday, but I'm not 100 percent convinced.
>
> My contractions never get super close together or consistent. But they are definitely the real and crampy kind.
>
> At 2:45 p.m., I call Mom and ask her to get ready just in case. "I'll call you at 3:15 with an update."
>
> My next three contractions are 17 minutes apart. "I'll call again at 4:00."
>
> This time I tell her to go ahead and come, but I'm still not sure I'm ready to go to the hospital.
>
> The five of us hold hands and pray and take off on our long trip to the hospital (three blocks away). I know I'm in labor but feel a little uneasy. Am I far enough along?
>
> I check in at the desk, and a nurse comes for me with a wheelchair. I feel very silly. I'm not even having contractions. I feel like I'm just posing as a woman in labor.
>
> I leave Mom, Livi, and Ava in the waiting room and go in the exam room with Gabe. Strip down to my socks, put on a lovely gown.
>
> "I need to be at least four centimeters," I tell Gabe.
>
> The nurse comes in to check me. "You're four to five," she says. "We'll call it five. You're not going anywhere."
>
> Hallelujah!

Gabe tells Mom and the girls the good news. They hook me up to monitors for a bit and then unhook them, and I walk to my suite, wrapped in a sheet, cords draped around my neck, sad that I didn't say a proper good-bye to my girlies.

I sit up in bed for a while, but Nina's heart rate monitor keeps beeping. She's acting all hyper and psychotic, itching to get out.

The nurse asks if I want to walk around for a while. I go visit my other babies in the waiting room.

Janelle (mom-in-law) has arrived. I hug and kiss Livi and Ava, talk, laugh, head back in. It's about 6:00 p.m. Rock (dad-in-law) wants to come. Janelle wants to know if I'll have the baby before he gets off work at 11:00. Uh, yes. Most definitely.

I get back to the room. The midwife comes to check me. Seven centimeters. She breaks my water, but there's no gush. Nina's head is low and blocking the canal.

She tells me I will be pleasantly surprised at the alertness of my baby without an epidural. (Paying for baby out-of-pocket means this is my first attempt to birth baby naturally.) She says I don't even need an IV—that will cut down on costs.

Gabe and I are having a wonderful time in the delivery room together, laughing and talking. My contractions became more intense, closer together. Totally bearable.

I just close my eyes, sit up straight, push my hands down into the mattress at my sides, pull my feet up toward my body, and rock back and forth. I don't make a peep. Just breathe calmly. And then it's over.

So I'm not exactly sure what time all hell breaks loose (a little after 7:00), but that is exactly what happens. I have a contraction. Stop. Breathe. Just like normal.

Then, all of a sudden, WHAM! I start to whimper and then cry. My body feels like it's exploding from every side. I don't know what to do.

Happy labor goes insane, that's what—the most action-packed ten minutes I will (hopefully) ever know.

"She's coming out!" I yell.

The nurse asks me to lie back so she can check me, but I can't. I can't move. I can't *not* move. I desperately need to find a way to move toward the pain—or move away from it—but I can't. It's *everywhere.* The nurse checks me while I'm sitting up.

"Complete," she said.

Yeah, no kidding. Complete *hell.*

Everybody comes rushing in at once—doctor, midwife, nurses, med students, secretaries, pizza guy. I am in sooo much pain. Whimpering like a puppy. Saying, *God, help me. God, help me.* Then *Help me, Jesus. Help me, Jesus.*

The doctor takes off the end of the table, scooches me back, I put my feet in the stirrups. I remember the overwhelming sensation of having to poop.

"I feel like I have to poop," I say brilliantly.

I want to curl up in a ball and die, not spread open my legs and invite the pain. I have one of Gabe's hands at my side and one above my head.

"It's going to feel like your bottom is splitting apart" the doctor says, "but it's not." Did he mean this statement to be *encouraging?* Goodness, I hope not.

He says I need to push through the pain and get it over with. "Some women get scared and stop pushing. Don't do that."

No, wouldn't want to do that. Push through the pain. Got it.

After the first push (OUCH!), he says he can see her head. "She has lots of brown hair." Again, how is this lessening the pain?

It hurts sooo bad. I don't expect to feel the pain everywhere—even in the very front of me, above where I pee. I ask the doctor, "Could you please take your hand off me?"

"That's not my hand," he says. "That's pressure from the baby's head."

Oh. Of course it is. I don't believe him.

Gabe looks down. Doc isn't lying. Gabe thinks this is a little funny. I actually do too, in a twisted sort of way.

The biggest, worst, awfullest part is getting her head out, obviously. HUGE relief when it pops out, but her shoulder is tough too. Once that pops out, she just slides out—and yea! I look down, help bring her up on me.

Pain forgotten. Just like they say will happen. I thought for sure that was a lie, but no. Unbelievable. I don't tear a bit.

She cries right away. They suction her out. My fluid is clear. No meconium.

"She's a girl!" Whew.

Lots of vernix coating. Long fingernails. Looks like Ava did. No conehead.

Daddy cuts the cord while I snap a picture.

I thank the doc. He says I can definitely go home in 24 hours. Even before, as long as the baby is doing okay. Lots of compliments for my controlled delivery.

"God answered your prayers."

"He always does."

"You could probably go home in four or five hours," he says.

I smile.

"You could probably even go work in the fields."

I beam.

I know there is no way I could ever go through that kind of pain again. Not for any amount of money. Not recommending natural childbirth to my friends.

Two days later I think, *That wasn't so bad. I could do it again.* Just shoot me.

Anywho, I am absolutely enamored by this tiny little creature. She is the most enchanting thing I have ever known.

Thank You, Jesus.

It's a Beautiful Thing

"A woman giving birth to a child has pain because her time has come;" the apostle John quotes Jesus as saying, "but when her baby is born she forgets the anguish because of her joy that a child is born into the world" (John 16:21). He hit the nail on the head.

Some people were just born to birth babies, like Rebecca. "I *love* delivery!" she says. "I had quick labors and pushed a total of eight times for the three children I birthed. I love the purposefulness of it. I love realizing how fabulous God designed our bodies so that we can bring new life into this world. I love the work involved and then the absolute relief and rejoicing once it is done."

"I hate being pregnant, but I *love* delivering a baby," says Cherith. "I'm crazy, I know. I love knowing that in an hour or two I'm going to be holding my baby for the first time. I love how close I feel to my husband during the labor and delivery and then especially afterward when we are with our new baby. I love the way I feel like I am the center of attention for a few hours. I love the concerned, helpless look in my husband's eyes when he sees how much pain I am in and knows he can't do anything to 'fix it.' It is the look of true love! I just love the whole experience, and I never really remember the pain."

"You work so hard to get that child out," says Kristen. "And in the end, you're rewarded with the most precious squirming miracle—that God hand-knit just for you. Meeting your child for the first time is a moment that is frozen in time forever."

Sweet Emotion

3

Bliss, Blues, and Blah

We're going to keep things relative here, okay? By that, I mean we're going to discuss the "bliss" part of the chapter at the very beginning and only for the briefest of moments. This is because the initial bliss you feel as a mother lasts for only the teensiest fraction of baby's first year (roughly 2 percent or less).

Remember the honeymoon period I referenced in the introduction? (If you skipped that part, go back and read it.) You come home from the hospital with your little bundle of angelicness, full of calm and peace and serenity, drinking in every detail of this captivating little person, hopelessly unaware that anything exists outside the bond the two of you have formed.

I love it when newbie moms (really new, as in one or two days new) tell me, "She is *such* a good baby. She sleeps all the time—she's already sleeping through the night—and she never cries unless she's hungry."

They positively glow while they relay this great news, and I haven't the heart to tell them what I've just told you—that with (most) every newborn comes a honeymoon period. It's part of the package. God designed it this way so that mothers wouldn't leave their babies at the hospital when it's time to go home.

So your baby is fabulous, every mother's dream. I know what you're saying. Even after three babies, I still haven't figured out how it is that you can love a tiny little person so much that your heart physically aches.

I remember being completely enchanted by my little newborns. I just wanted to hold them and stare at them and never, ever let them out of my sight. I loved them so much I could have eaten them. I loved them so much I could have bawled. And often did. I didn't want them to ever be more than single-digits days old. Never.

Pure bliss.

And yet, all good things must come to an end. The euphoric, enamored state doesn't last. It usually comes to a screeching halt in fact.

Before you can blink, your stay is up at your island resort, and it's back to work. Except that you've started a new job. And you work 168 hours a week with no overtime pay. Er, no pay at all actually. In fact, *you* pay at this job.

Oh, sure, there are blissful moments throughout baby's entire first year. Lots and lots of them. There are even snatches of parenting bliss throughout your child's entire life. But once you reach the end of that honeymoon stage, there are no extended periods of parenting bliss, and especially not in that first transition year.

Bliss is defined as "ecstasy, euphoria, supreme happiness and contentment, the joy of heaven." And perpetual bliss this side of eternity is an oxymoron.

Please hear what I'm saying, my friend. I am *not* saying that parenthood isn't one of the most awesome things you'll ever be a part of. Rather, I'm saying that "bliss" isn't an accurate descriptor.

We live in a fallen world, and parenting is a gritty task. Rewarding, fulfilling, magical, beautiful, incomparable, indescribable, wondrous, and joyous? Absolutely. Blissful? No.

Sweet Euphoria

As I type these words, my friend Abby is freshly home from the hospital with her tiny little girl. I've loved peeking in on her blog these past two weeks. When she finds time to write, she just gushes about her precious baby. She and her little one are on cloud nine. Here's a sampling of her blog:

> She is such a good baby and is feeding so great. The first night home she slept two four-hour periods. Right now Daddy and baby are sound asleep on the couch...

> Motherhood is amazing. I have loved everything about being a mom so far. My daughter amazes me every day with every little face she makes, and just watching her sleep brings such joy. I never knew how much I could love someone without even really knowing them, but the moment she was put in my arms I felt in love...

> I have been feeling great, still taking it easy but doing some things to get out of the house...

> I'm getting ready to feed Ali so this will be fast, but still everything is going great! Today is Drew's last day home all day with us. It has been a great two weeks.

She posted a quick update today and apologized for not catching up on everyone else's blogs. And then she said the cutest thing. "It's just that if I had to pick Xanga or my baby, I pick my baby!"

We'll see how things go over the next few weeks and months. This friend is the latest of many who have had babies in the past year and blogged about their mommy-life from day one. So far, the patterns have been nearly identical.

Ready, ready, ready for baby to come. Baby comes. Bliss ensues. Then come the blues.

Take Jessica B. and Kristen for example—two dear friends who were so kind to have adorable baby boys right as I was beginning this book. The little guys were kid number two for both gals. And both Jess and Kristen experienced a honeymoon period like I've talked about.

They'd say things like how blissful life was, how easy their babies were, how perfect life was, stuff like that.

So did I tell these darling souls that the honeymoon wouldn't last? Heavens no. I knew they'd figure it out on their own soon enough.

I just smiled like a Grinning Gertie and said things like, "I hope he keeps it up for you, the little angel. And he's so darn cute too. You're one blessed mama."

Short-Term Memory

If you expected bliss with your first baby and it didn't last, you'd think that you might know better the second time around. This isn't always the case.

My friend Colleen is mom to not one, not two, but three little girls. Yet when she brought baby number three home from the hospital, she had sky-high expectations for life as a third-time mom. She says she's convinced God makes us forget what it's like so we'll keep having babies.

Here's her story:

> I imagined this blissful situation where my little angel baby would lay down to sleep without crying and not awake until the allotted two-hour nap was complete. Then I would gracefully feed my lovey, she would play contentedly for at least an hour, and then I would lay her back down for another two-hour nap. This would continue throughout the day…Then at night, she would just close her precious eyes, droop off into la-la land, and not awaken for at least five or six hours.
>
> I would be able to keep the house spotless, scrapbook, blog, play with the older girls, go on dates with my husband…
>
> Wake up to reality! I forgot how much babies need their mommies. I'm starting all over again, and sometimes I just want my freedom back.
>
> I'm still learning. I'm trying to savor the moments. I'm impatient though. I get frustrated when I can't calm her. I'm scared about the possibility of another colicky or acid

reflux baby. I'm scared of sleep training. I'm scared of being a failure. *Lord, help me! I need You!*

The Afterbirth Aftershocks

Don't you just love people who think things like morning sickness and PMS are figments of the imagination? Or that there's some way to avoid them just by putting your mind to it? If you're of that sort of opinion, please don't share it with me.

I had a woman tell me once that "morning sickness is all in a woman's head." Are you kidding me? Just because *you* didn't suffer from it? Tell that to my friend Missy, who spent most of her pregnancy hooked up to an IV for 20 hours a day. Or another friend who vomited every day for eight months.

I did used to question whether my premenstrual grouchiness was a bit mental on my part. During those many months of trying to get pregnant, I knew my monthly cycle like the back of my hand. So, I knew exactly when my period would be starting. I often wondered if I was just looking for an excuse to have a bad attitude.

But when I'm not trying to conceive, I don't have a clue what's going on. I pay no attention. My period creeps up on me from out of nowhere. Just today, I felt really crappy. Sad, tired, in a funk. I even told my husband, "It feels like there's some sort of demonic oppression around me." He looked at me like I was bonkers and essentially told me to suck it up.

Then, just a few moments ago, I exited the bathroom with a grin on my face. "No demons," I said. "Just my period."

All that to say that a woman's hormones can do crazy things to her mind and body. And building a baby in your womb for nine months, pushing it out, and trying to recover from the whole mess can wreak havoc on your hormones.

Postpartum blues are the real deal. Of course, women suffer from it in varying degrees. I never had full-blown depression, but I certainly struggled emotionally in a way I wasn't used to and that I couldn't control.

I haven't done the scientific research. I don't know exactly what's going on with all those raging hormones in your body when you're pregnant and then after you give birth. But in addition to all that, you've got the sleep deprivation and the hugest transition you've ever had to make in your life. Bar none.

You didn't want to be one of "those" women—the women who suffer from postpartum issues. But this little hormonal adjustment deal is no respecter of persons. It's not a sign of weakness. And there are a thousand different facets to it. So let me just share a few stories from some moms who have been in the postbirthing trenches.

First, I asked moms to describe their postpartum experience in one- or two-word sentences. I'd imagine you'll find an adjective or two you can call your own.

> "Happy! Then sad. Happy! Then sad. Up! Down. Over and over!"
>
> "Euphoric. Percocet-clouded. Tiring. Fabulous."
>
> "Worried. Cried a lot."
>
> "Very emotional. Feeling overwhelmed."
>
> "Frustration, exhaustion, complete happiness, love."
>
> "Joy. Overwhelming work. Exhaustion."
>
> "Physical aftermath. Rebounded slowly."
>
> "Rewarding. Exhausting. Painful. Challenging. Prayer filled."
>
> "Guilt. Soreness. Unexpected feelings. Emotional."
>
> "Scary. Lonely. Incapable. Fear. Powerlessness."
>
> "Overwhelming responsibility. Cried frequently."
>
> "Sleep deprived. Starving constantly. Sweet little newborn cries."
>
> "Dense fog."
>
> "Relaxing. Exciting. Scary. Humbling. Perfect."

"Weepy for a couple weeks."

"Surreal. Up and down."

"Depression. Sadness. Exhaustion. Alone."

"Out of control. Lonely. Trapped."

"Initially blissful. Then depression."

"Painful. Bloody, awful mess."

"Shell-shocked. Turned inside out. Swept away. In a fog. Delirious."

"Cold chills. Total exhaustion. Very hungry."

"Overwhelming. Confusing. A letdown."

"Hell on earth."

You love your little baby. He brings you more joy than you could have imagined. Your love for him is so intense. And sometimes the intensity hurts. Is this what it's like to be a mother? Will you always feel like this? It's all so overwhelming.

It's almost as if you want him to get bigger quickly so your love and concern for him will ease up. But will it? Surely it must. You can't handle this kind of intensity indefinitely—it's enough to kill you. You feel as if you've been overtaken by a force you didn't know existed.

Your thoughts begin to wander. You think back to just a few weeks ago when you were still pregnant. Suddenly, a wave of sadness passes over you, and you feel a sense of loss. You miss being pregnant. That part of your life was so beautiful, so special, and so fleeting. You miss your round, tight belly. You miss feeling your little baby twist and turn and roll and kick and hiccup. You miss that thrill of anticipation—what will our baby look like? Is he a boy, or is she a girl?

And yes, you miss the attention. The admiring looks you got. The way everybody catered to your every need. No one really cares about you anymore. All eyes are on the little person who used to occupy your womb.

Being home by yourself with your newborn is harder than you could have imagined. Your first time alone you just cried and cried. You cry every night when your husband comes home from work. You cry in the middle of the night when you can't get your baby to go back to sleep. You cry when breast-feeding is a hundred times harder than you'd ever imagined.

You're sick and tired of crying.

Real Moms

My friend Krysty didn't suffer from postpartum depression per se. "Just high frustration from not knowing how to 'do life' with a baby in tow," she says. "I wanted normal life back as quickly as possible. I didn't realize that 'normal' would have an entirely new definition."

What were some of the rough spots for her? "Trying to figure out when to nurse him and get somewhere before he needed to eat again. Figuring out how to put him in that stupid Baby Björn. I thought I was in the circus or something."

My cousin Kyla had similar feelings. "Getting him ready was a huge challenge in the beginning. There's so much to do to get a newborn ready to go somewhere. And once he's bathed and dressed and fed and his bag is packed, you look at yourself and realize you're braless and appear as though you've been hit by a truck."

My friend Anne Marie remembers lots and lots of tears. "On day two or three, when my milk came in," she said, "I literally couldn't stop crying. It was a horrible out-of-control feeling. I knew I was so happy, but I felt so sad. I called my practitioner to see if I needed medicines because I was frightened, but I felt better within two weeks."

My friend Kristen can relate to the whole honeymoon analogy—smooth sailing, smooth sailing, and then crash!

> For two whole weeks after my second child was born, I was trucking along, loving life and thinking I had such a great handle on everything. I thought I had been dealt a perfect wild card and all was right with the world.

Then week three hit. My older son got sick, the baby got fussy, feeding problems started, and exhaustion set in. Seriously, for the first time in my life I felt lucky to get a shower in and really lucky to get my breakfast eaten in one sitting, and all my dreams of a clean house had been forsaken.

I had to admit that the adjustment wasn't easy anymore—and that I wasn't handling it perfectly. That sometimes the baby would scream and I didn't have any idea why. That I needed to call the lactation consultant because my baby couldn't get through a feeding without choking, swallowing too much air, puking almost everything up, and screaming his head off because his belly hurt. That I felt run ragged and totally consumed by breast pumps, cough medicine, puke bowls, laundry, and everyday life.

Then Kristen came down with a fever and chills that turned out to be mastitis—a breast infection. Every bone and muscle in her body ached. "I writhed in pain in bed, crying that it just wasn't fair."

She survived. And somehow in that great paradox of motherhood, Kristen says in spite of it all, she felt so thankful. "I love our new family. I was tired, so tired, and so overwhelmed. But I felt blessed—in a thousand and one ways."

The Whole Truth

Another dear friend of mine, whose second child was two months old, was watching TV with her husband. A woman on the show was talking about having another kid. "Don't do it!" my friend said to the actress. "It's too hard!"

In his calm, firm manner, Hubby said she shouldn't be telling people how hard it is. At a party the previous weekend, she had said something similar to some folks during a casual conversation. They asked how things were going. She gave them an honest answer. Hubby thought maybe the whole truth didn't always need to be told.

My friend begged to differ. "I thought that was horrible advice. I wish I would have had some warning! I wouldn't have given the baby back or anything. Just give me some fair warning that it's a tough transition!"

Thanks to my friend for having this "friendly discussion" with her better half. This is part of the reason I'm writing this book. To give you fair warning and prepare you for how rough it can be. Not to complain, whine, play martyr, or beef about my life as a mom, but to tell the truth. It's hard. Very, very hard. And the stinkin'est best thing you'll ever do in life. You can find joy in the struggles. So dig in your heels and get some of that joy! It's no picnic, but you don't want to miss it for the world.

My friend and her hubby fought, kissed, and made up that night. (Well, they fought and made up. I don't really know about the kissing part.)

"I was really ticked off at first," she says. "I felt like he didn't understand at all how tough the transition was for me. He just wanted me to snap out of it and be happy. Change my thinking. Yeah, right."

But in the end, that "conversation" was the turning point of her postpartum experience. Hubby gave her lots of good insight and acknowledged the fact that she was having a really hard time. He even suggested that she get some help or meds.

"It's been getting better since then," says my friend. "I think just having him realize and admit that something big was going on with my emotions helped tremendously. I felt like he was part of the team and not on the outside telling me that my feelings were petty and that I should just fix them on my own. I felt a little less alone."

Reading Between the Lines

Another dear friend shared some thoughts on expectations with me that I'd say are fairly universal among new moms. I'll let her share them in her own delightful words.

> You know all of those fab pregnancy magazines the doctor gives you? And all those books you read about being a new

parent? Well, they all tell us that moms need to take it easy for the first few weeks, right? You know what I'm talking about—dads should field the phone calls, in-laws should not drop in at all hours, grandmas don't know everything about the new baby, mom needs rest, husbands should take over the upkeep of the house for a little while, and yada, yada.

Well, I've been so bugged about this lately because it sounds rosy, but unless other people besides new moms are reading those books, all they do is get the new moms' hopes up and lead them to expect stuff that doesn't happen.

I have a solution. Expectant and new moms need to either (a) highlight sections of books that talk about the help we need and pass it around to hubby, grandma, friends, and relatives or (b) actually communicate these expectations with people that might be around when the new baby comes.

I'll ashamedly admit that, eight months later, I still have little annoyed thoughts creep into my head—especially toward my husband. Like, *Man! He even let me cook him dinner three days after delivery!*

See, I wanted to play that game. I wanted to start dinner, and then I wanted him to come into the kitchen and say, "Oh, no! Sweetie, you can't cook! You just had a baby! Here, go out there and put your feet up. Where's the recipe card? I'll cook it. And I'll make cookies too!"

Didn't happen.

I had all of these expectations in my head (that's what the magazines said!), but I didn't communicate them at all. My husband didn't read those magazines. And it didn't really work in my favor. If only I'd spoken.

Next time I have a baby, I'm going to put as much work into my postbirth plan as I did my birth plan.

Climbing out of the Pit

When I first started writing this book, my friend Jessica C. shared her struggles with postpartum depression with me. She was fresh from the battlefield and told me her story straight from her gut.

"Use whatever you can to help other women," she told me. "I know God had me go through all that for a reason."

Just looking at Jess would show you that PPD is no respecter of persons. On the outside, she looks like she's got it all together. A Jennifer Aniston look-alike complete with the long, brown hair, perfect makeup, and impeccable taste in clothes, she's thin and curvy in all the right places. And if that doesn't make you want to puke, she's a sweet, caring girl who loves the Lord with all her heart.

When Jess gave birth to her first child, Austin, last January, her perfect world caved in on her.

"I felt guilty about everything," she says, "and it was a deep and heavy guilt. I felt guilty if I needed to sleep. I felt guilty if I propped my baby in his Boppy instead of cuddling him close. I felt guilty because I couldn't nurse him. I felt guilty when I was pumping eight times a day and loathing every minute of it. I had read the books that said, 'Think of your precious baby and envision his face while you pump for a good milk supply,' and I felt guilty that I hated these plastic things attached to a machine."

She said she even remembers telling someone that the pump was talking to her. "When I would get up at 4:00 a.m. and lean against the couch and pump, I felt that the sound of the machine was saying, 'Black hole.' Not very uplifting, I know!"

The first few times Jess took Austin to the doctor, she ended up in tears. "My doctor finally had to tell me to get a grip because it would affect my baby. I felt guilty for not wanting to hold him all the time. I felt guilty that I couldn't cook dinner and take care of him."

She couldn't think. She couldn't remember how much he'd eaten and when. She couldn't return phone calls or host friends who wanted to see her baby.

"The floor had literally fallen out of my life," Jess says. "I had hit rock bottom and was completely a puddle of empty emotions. I felt so guilty that this was supposed to be one of the happiest times in my life and I was just a mess."

Family members would say, "Oh, you are so nice to let other people hold him," and Jess would think, *That's because I don't know what to do with him!*

She didn't enjoy play groups with masses of other moms. "I felt like I was missing the 'mommy gene,'" she says. "I remember wanting to scream when friends with older babies told me it got better. I didn't know *how* it would get better. I couldn't even get through the next hour."

When Jess shared this with me, her son was five months old, and her story had a happy ending. No, being a mom isn't a piece of cake, but God delivered her out of the pit of depression.

"When I look at Austin, I know it was all worth it," Jess says. "But the unknown was scary. Very scary. I was so glad that I have a very big God, because He heard my daily cries—*God, I can't do this today!* or *God, please help me!*"

Jess says she's doing great now. "I still have challenging days. I'm still in that raw state of being. But I also feel like that time was so amazing for me because as my memory came back and I started to be able to think, I really saw how reliant I was on God. I needed Him desperately to get me through one day, even one hour, at a time."

She says she even yearns sometimes for those mornings of stumbling out of bed at 4:00 a.m. to feed Austin or check on him. Then when she couldn't go back to sleep, she'd read psalm after psalm after psalm, and they soothed her soul.

"I just pray my story can help other moms who are experiencing the same things. I know I had so many friends who told me they felt crazy, just like I did. I've always believed that God uses our dark days to help others to get through theirs."

What a great thing to believe, because it comes straight from God's Word. "Praise be to the God and Father of our Lord Jesus Christ, the Father of compassion and the God of all comfort, who comforts us in all our troubles, so that we can comfort those in any trouble with the comfort we ourselves have received from God" (2 Corinthians 1:3-4).

Marissa has a story to share as well. Her son was three months old when she finally realized she had postpartum depression. Her sisters both had it, and depression runs in her family. Coupled with some tough life circumstances at the time, it was almost inevitable. Marissa's mom "diagnosed" her long-distance over the phone. She encouraged her to tell her doctor and get help.

"The problem was that my husband did not believe (at the time) in taking medication for depression," Marissa shares. "So, in the midst of the worst of my depression, I was trying to work through that in my marriage. By God's grace, it got bad enough that my husband decided it was okay, although he was upset about it. We've since gotten counseling and worked through that."

Marissa acknowledges that medication may not be the answer for everyone's depression, but hers had gotten bad enough (with hopelessness and suicidal thoughts) that "I needed it in order to get to any place where I could work through my problems."

Praise the Lord for medical advances and brilliant doctors in the field who can help women get back on their feet after such a difficult ordeal. And praise Him for women like Jessica and Marissa who have a heart to share their experiences in hopes of blessing other moms.

The Hardest Part

If a mother tells you the first year of parenting was easier than she thought it would be, either she's a big fat liar or she has a lousy memory. Harsh? Perhaps. But a truer word has ne'er been written.

Even if you don't ever suffer from PPD, being a mom to a newborn is just physically, mentally, and emotionally tough. Draining. Exhausting. Frustrating. Grueling. (I could come up with an adjective for every letter of the alphabet if you'd like.)

I asked women to share the hardest part of having a newborn. Most of them had trouble choosing just one thing. If you're in those trenches right now, take comfort in these words of empathy from your fellow moms. If your little one has already moved from newborn to plain old baby, just grin big, pat yourself on the back, and think, "Man, that's a lot of stuff I survived!"

I asked moms, in your personal and humble opinion, what is the most difficult part of being a mom to a newborn?

"Sleep deprivation, hands down!" says Jessica B. "Learning to live with the 24/7 demands of a baby. Feeling confident in my decisions despite the advice of others. The emotions I didn't know how to handle. In general, sleep deprivation is a killer. I think any negative thing is magnified by the lack of sleep. Everything seems so much worse."

"Realizing babies do not have a formula to make them do what they are 'supposed' to do," says Tracy. "And being humble enough to ask for help."

"The hardest part is just before they started sleeping through the night well," says one woman. "Around that ten-week mark, I remember feeling like I would die!"

"Fighting with my husband," Jessica C. says. "We were both so overwhelmed. He would come home from work, and I felt like a maniac. We had a week of me literally freaking out for an hour or two every night!"

"Sleep deprivation and not knowing if you are making the right decisions for your child," says Lindsey. "You get so much unwanted advice from others. I took a while to realize that every child's personality is different. What worked for my friend's easygoing baby was not going to work for my two type A babies."

"Lack of sleep and trying to get a routine down," says Casey. "And when you nurse (which I absolutely loved), you feel like that's all you do. And when you get in bed with your husband at night, you feel over-touched already, and you just don't want to be touched any more."

"There is no break," my friend Missy says. "Everything else in life you can take a day off from, go on vacation from, but not a baby. No matter how sick you are, how tired you feel, you have a little person that can't be left alone and needs pretty constant care. I had a stomach bug shortly after having Leah, and it hit me—I still had to nurse her and care for her. I would not be able to just lie around and get better. I just prayed that I would be able to make it through each nursing session without having to run to the bathroom."

"I really struggled with the change from being Megan to being Mommy," one woman said. "My whole life pre-baby had revolved around me, and now it revolved around someone else. It was hard to feed the baby every feeding and miss out on things going on around me."

"The lack of sleep is a bear," says Molly. "Then there's always the fear of doing something wrong or harmful to this tiny child."

"Having a colicky baby takes all the joy out of the first few weeks of mommy life," says Michelle. "The day she cried for 13 hours straight was absolutely the most challenging."

"Trying to breast-feed," said one woman. "No one tells you that the baby is always hungry and that breast-feeding is so time-consuming. Once I fed her, burped her, and got her back to sleep, she would be hungry again in an hour. I felt lonely and frustrated because I was the only one who could feed her. At times it was a great bonding experience, and other times I felt like my husband was getting off easy."

"I was used to freedom and gallivanting around wherever and whenever," says Courtney. "Now I have an extra appendage."

"I am always so tired!" one woman said. "My body is just not how it's supposed to be. My breasts hurt, my stomach is gross, I feel so dirty in my girl parts from all the blood and nastiness coming out. But the exhaustion is the worst."

"It was much more difficult than I ever imagined," admits my friend Kristen. "I had wanted children my entire life, but when it actually happened I was unprepared for the total responsibility that would fall on my shoulders and the work involved. I just thought I would dress him up and take him out so people could ohh and ahh at him. I didn't think about sleepless nights, night terrors, sickness, eating problems, and stuff like that."

"I think, at some point, everyone I knew held my breast to try to help my daughter latch on," said one woman. "No modesty left."

"I gave up on breast-feeding very early," one woman said, "and battled extreme guilt for a long time regarding the decision."

"Finding time to sleep," says my friend Suzanne. "Finding time to make myself look pretty. Getting rid of diaper rashes. Gritting my teeth through the initial week of breast-feeding. Changing a diaper without getting peed or pooped on."

"The complete change of lifestyle," one woman told me. "No matter how prepared you think you are, you're never prepared to care for a tiny new human being 24 hours a day, 7 days a week."

Wow—I need a nap just from reading all that. Yet the awesome thing is that as hard as motherhood is, it is one of the most incredible things you'll ever do. And God will give you the strength not just to endure it but to thrive on being a mommy.

The Best Comfort of All

I just love encouragement. I love being encouraged. I love encouraging others. And I'm so thankful for the opportunity to share some words of comfort and inspiration with you in the coming pages.

Other moms are a fabulous source of encouragement, sure, but God is our ultimate Comforter. He knows us more intimately than we know ourselves and is the only One who knows exactly what we need in every life situation.

The Bible is full of thousands of verses that will comfort your mommy soul as you read them and take them to heart. Books can be great, but they are no substitute for God's Word.

Jamie found encouragement in Psalm 91:4-5: "He will cover you with his feathers, and under his wings you will find refuge; his faithfulness will be your shield and rampart. You will not fear the terror of night, nor the arrow that flies by day."

"I love this verse because it is so visual!" she says. "The imagery of being under His care is just so comforting. And I love verse 5 as it talks about not fearing the terror of night, which I saw as not fearing the sleepless nights of a newborn. And not fearing the arrow that flies by day, which I saw as not fearing the long days all by myself with my children while my husband is at work."

Marissa was comforted by 1 Peter 5:6-11, which an older mom gave to her when she was battling postpartum depression. Verse 7 is a familiar one: "Cast all your anxiety on him because he cares for you." And verse 10 says, "And the God of all grace, who called you to his eternal glory in Christ, after you have suffered a little while, will himself restore you and make you strong, firm and steadfast."

"To be honest," Marissa admits, "she gave them to me written out on an index card inside a greeting card. At the time we had no income and selfishly, I was half hoping that maybe the card had a gift of money in it. I realize now that what she gave me was worth far more than gold or silver. I found those verses at a later time when I really needed them. I knew that God was speaking to me, telling me that He Himself would make me 'strong, firm and steadfast.' I clung to that, and those verses helped to bring me out of the depression."

"I love Isaiah 40:31," says Jessica C. " 'But those who hope in the LORD will renew their strength. They will soar on wings like eagles; they will run and not grow weary, they will walk and not be faint.' "

"This verse was so important to me when we thought our infant son might have cystic fibrosis. We had to wait a week for the second test results to come in. We had people all over the country praying for him and fasting. I kept thinking of this verse. The day before we got the results in, a bald eagle flew over our house. Austin is perfectly healthy today."

So many moms mentioned that they love Isaiah 40:11. It's one of my favorites as well. The NIV says, "He tends his flock like a shepherd: He gathers the lambs in his arms and carries them close to his heart; he gently leads those that have young."

Those that have young—that's you!—have a special place in God's heart. He knows how hard it is, and He's going to lead you ever so gently during this fragile time.

The Message version of the verse is really cool too. "Like a shepherd, he will care for his flock, gathering the lambs in his arms, hugging them as he carries them, leading the nursing ewes to good pasture."

I can just picture Him lovingly leading you to a peaceful place where all your needs are met.

Your children will deplete you of all kinds of natural resources—milk, time, energy—but God will lead you to good pasture and fill you back up! While you're busy caring for the needs of that precious little baby, He's going to care for your every need.

Hundreds and hundreds of verses in the Bible can give you a lot of encouragement during this unparalleled time in your life. Never, ever underestimate God's living, breathing Word and the way it can bless and soothe and strengthen your weary mommy heart.

4

Be Still, My Heart

Surprises and doubts, fears and dreams—that's what motherhood is made of. Sugar and spice, snips and snails, sure, but oh, there is so much more to being a mom!

What surprised you most about motherhood? What kinds of things caught you off guard? What is harder than you thought? Is anything easier? How does your new reality compare with the mental picture you used to have of motherhood?

What doubts do you have? Do you often feel as if you're lacking in wisdom? Do you sometimes feel that you just don't have what it takes to be a good mom?

What about your fears? What kinds of things scare you now that you have a child? What do you find yourself anxious over and concerned about? Having a child multiplies any fears you may have had before—and you'll have fears you never knew existed.

And what about your hopes and dreams? We're dreamers by nature. We long for a reality that is blissful and romantic, fulfilling and enchanting. In fact, heaven is what we truly crave, but God in His goodness gives us glimpses of eternity here on earth. What do you dream for your child as he grows?

Full of Surprises

I love asking moms—especially new ones—what surprised them most about motherhood. They're usually quick to answer. I've yet to find a woman who could honestly say, "Being a mom was exactly how I thought it would be—nothing more, nothing less."

The way motherhood plays out in our minds is rarely how it turns out in real life. Daydreams always include a best-case scenario (as we know it). We don't even think to envision anything less than the romantic ideal.

What I love about these moms' answers is that they're a perfect combination of "I didn't realize it would be so hard" and "I didn't know it would be so wonderful."

That's motherhood for ya.

So, tell me, friend, what surprised you most about becoming a mom?

> "The deep level of emotions I feel and how contrasting they can be at times—love, frustration, loneliness, joy, anger, appreciation, failure."

> "I am amazed that I have so much love for each of my girls. I was afraid after my second was born that I wouldn't be able to love her as much as I loved my first."

> "How the days seem to creep by but the years tend to fly."

> "How in love and devoted you can be to one little person. My husband always tells me I need to do something for myself, but I don't like to be away from her."

> "The emotions that come with it. In one word, they're fierce. My daughter has had a lot of medical testing, and so often I feel a strong instinct to jump in there and take the pain for her. When she's sweet and funny, I love her so strongly, it catches me off guard at times. When others do things that could hurt her, I feel a burning anger and protectiveness."

"How early on we could see her personality coming out."

"How complicated life gets once you have a child. I think in a totally different manner than I did before I was a mom regarding priorities and the way I go about daily tasks. How did moms function before bouncers and swings and strollers?"

"The fear. I had no idea how much my heart would scream at the thought of something happening to my little girl. I can't even watch a story on the news about an abandoned child without crying and getting angry."

"I had very high ideals that I wanted to follow and found that very little goes according to plan when you involve a child."

"The bond I share with my daughters. I did not grow up in a close family, and my girls and I are constantly snuggling and hugging."

"That I am more like my mother than I ever knew."

"I am surprised by how much I worry about their eternal destiny, by the need I feel to lie in bed at night and plead with God for their salvation."

"That there are no breaks. Even when she's with someone else or asleep or not needing my full attention, I'm still thinking about her, wanting to be with her, and feeling responsible for her. I'm amazed when I realize that I'll probably feel this way to some degree for the rest of my life."

"I think it is hard to put into words how rewarding it is. Seeing my child go through each new phase of life is so gratifying. I never realized how much love I could have for another human being. It is different from the love I have for my husband, and I'm not sure I could pinpoint how."

"That, as a mother, you will never get a vacation as long as your children are with you. You will always be on duty."

"I was surprised at my instant bond with other mothers, even those I don't know."

When in Doubt

Surprises can be cool. Doubts—not so much. Doubting yourself as a mom is normal. After all, this is the first time you've done something like this motherhood thing.

One friend told me she had doubts in the area of training her children to live for Christ. "I'm afraid of unintentionally teaching them worldly values because of my lack of spiritual discipline," she said.

Another friend doubted her ability to remember everything a mom needs to do when raising a child. "I just feel like I'm going to forget something really important while raising my son!" she said.

"I am most anxious that my children will not feel confident in their abilities," says one mom. "I am a shy person who struggles with insecurities, and my mom wasn't a confident person either. I fear that I'll pass on my lack of self-confidence."

How do I know if I'm doing this right? How do I know which advice to take and which to toss? How in the world am I ever going to be a good mom?

Doubts are normal, but they don't need to characterize our lives. The truth is this: We *are* inadequate. We have every reason to feel insecure in our ability to be good moms.

And you'll quickly find that people all around you have "wisdom" to share—and much of that wisdom will be offered unsolicited. There is definitely a time and place to get advice from others—your mom, friends with kids, books. But God's Word tells us where we should ultimately look for wisdom.

James 1:5 says, "If any of you lacks wisdom, he should ask God, who gives generously to all without finding fault, and it will be given to him."

I love this same verse in The Message. "If you don't know what you're doing, pray to the Father. He loves to help. You'll get his help, and won't be condescended to when you ask for it."

Maybe this verse speaks to me so loudly because I spend a lot of time not knowing what I'm doing. And I love the fact that God's not going to laugh at my stupid questions.

So the Bible doesn't tell you how often to bathe your baby or how long she can sit in her bouncy seat without feeling neglected, but a lot of wisdom is in there nonetheless.

It is absolutely biblical to come to God and ask Him for wisdom, for help, for tangible, concrete answers to life's problems. I'm not talking about God appearing to you in a dream or speaking audibly in your ear. I'm talking about crying out in need to your Father—and seeing your prayers answered in all kinds of ways. Oh, if we would only pour our hearts out to the Lord constantly. He has so many blessings to pour into our lives.

We serve a God who has more than enough power to do anything and everything. He knows everything. Whatever we need in our roles as moms, He promises to provide. All we have to do is ask and believe He'll answer. And we have to spend time digging into His Word.

I can think of three reasons why God didn't specifically spell out parenting instructions in the Bible.

1. He wants us to go to Him daily in prayer and then trust Him to give us the wisdom we've asked for (James 1:6-7).

2. Part of His plan is for us to ask others for help. Proverbs 11:14 (MSG) says, "Without good direction, people lose their way; the more wise counsel you follow, the better your chances." (Of course, you still need to pray for wisdom. Not everybody out there offering advice is the sharpest crayon in the box.)

3. God has given us so much freedom. What works for your baby or marriage or family may not work for someone else. God didn't make us out of cookie cutters, and He doesn't expect us to act as if He did. We have so much room for uniqueness and creativity and differences—especially in raising children.

And just when you get really good at one part of mothering, your little one moves into brand-new territory. As she gets older, the number of choices you have to make as a mom seems to grow exponentially.

Spirit Smarts

I'm far from being a Bible expert. But I'm learning new truths all the time, and on good days, I hungrily gulp down delicious morsels from God's Word. What a difference a little (or a lot of) help from the Holy Spirit makes.

I've had friends lament that they wish they'd been born smarter, but God is less worried about intelligence than about wisdom. He promises that each and every believer has everything she needs to live a life of godliness. When it comes to being a mom, your IQ matters far less than your willingness to ask for wisdom and listen to the Holy Spirit.

We place quite a premium on intellect in this day and age, but a lot of smarty-pants people are out there with tons of head knowledge and no idea how to put it to practical use.

Make sure you hear this—we have all been given the same Spirit when it comes to interpreting biblical truth. Our ACT score (or whether or not we even took the test) is irrelevant. I'm embarrassed to admit that I took years to ask for divine understanding. I was relying on my own intelligence, which, in God's economy, isn't worth what I thought it was.

I began to notice verses all over the place that spoke to this phenomenon. In Psalm 119, verses 98-100, the psalmist talks about being wiser than his enemies, his teachers, his elders—all because he meditates on God's statutes. Wisdom has little to do with IQ. It's something God promises to give to any child of His who asks for it.

Jesus said, "I praise you, Father, Lord of heaven and earth, because you have hidden these things from the wise and learned, and revealed them to little children. Yes, Father, for this was your good pleasure" (Matthew 11:25-26).

"Open my eyes that I may see wonderful things in your law," says Psalm 119:18. It isn't about our own knowledge and intellect. It's about God answering an honest and faith-filled prayer that our eyes will be opened.

Verse 130 reads, "The unfolding of your words gives light; it gives understanding to the simple." That's what we like to hear.

"Trust God from the bottom of your heart; don't try to figure out everything on your own. Listen for God's voice in everything you do, everywhere you go; he's the one who will keep you on track" (Proverbs 3:5-6 MSG).

The Bible's truths aren't there to be uncovered by the brilliant few; they're there to be revealed by God to a heart committed to loving and knowing Him.

They are there for you and me.

Eugene Peterson's introduction to the book of Proverbs in The Message describes what wisdom is in a tangible way.

"Wisdom is the art of living skillfully in whatever actual conditions we find ourselves." He says that it has to do with becoming skilled in our everyday tasks and relationships—which include raising our children.

"Threaded through all these items is the insistence that the way we think and respond to God is the most practical thing we do. In matters of everyday practicality, nothing, absolutely nothing, takes precedence over God."

God's Word is alive. It will speak to your very core if you let it. If you're not interested in what God's Word has to say about life and parenting, go ahead and skip or skim over those parts. But I'll warn you that the Bible permeates my mothering (at least, that's my ultimate goal). My prayer is that in every decision I make as a mom, I will think the way God teaches me to in His Word.

A collection of my own advice and opinions is lovely, I'm sure, but my words only have power when they're backed up with Scripture. Before you read any further in this book or in any parenting book, ask God to simply open your heart to the wisdom in His Word. Filter other people's words through His.

Anxiety and Fear

Fear plagues us all at one time or another. For some of us, it's pretty much all the time. And as any mom will tell you, fears for your children are far more difficult to deal with than fears for yourself.

I remember a very real fear I had about a month before my first child was born. *Lord,* I wrote in my journal, *I've been struggling lately with an irrational fear that You're going to take Gabe away from me and that I'll have to raise my baby without a father.*

I would lie in bed or sit in a chair and let my mind wander to all sorts of horrifying scenarios. I would even start crying, as if it had really happened and my husband wasn't in the next room over, sitting at his computer.

And of course, I'd also worry about something happening to the little baby I already loved so much. I finally realized that living a life of fear wasn't going to work. I couldn't even enjoy the blessings God had given me. I was so scared they'd be taken away.

I finally just pleaded with Him, *Lord, help me to give Gabe and our baby completely to You. As scared as I am, I know that You won't take either of them from this earth a single second before their appointed time. And if You do take them, You will provide the strength I need to carry on—somehow, some way. Please help me give them to You!*

I found verses that spoke to my fears and comforted my soul. Just like Hannah, I had prayed and prayed for a baby. When she finally had Samuel, she said, "For this child I prayed, and the LORD has granted me my petition which I asked of Him. Therefore I have also lent him to the LORD; as long as he lives he shall be lent to the LORD" (1 Samuel 1:27-29 NKJV).

Her words gave me the courage to lend my baby to God. Or even better, realize that this little one was on loan to me from her heavenly Father.

And to think that God loved my child even more than I did. "If you then, being evil, know how to give good gifts to your children," Jesus said, "how much more will your Father who is in heaven give good things to those who ask him!" (Matthew 7:11 NKJV).

If you thought you had fears when you were pregnant, they weren't nothin' compared to how you felt after that little one entered the world.

When Olivia wasn't even a week old, I was overcome by an almost paralyzing fear. I remember the physical pain in my chest from being so scared.

I wrote this in my journal:

> Something strange is going on inside of me. It has two parts. (1) I do not want to leave Olivia—not even for a second. And (2) I don't want to take her out anywhere for anything.
>
> I'm talking really strong feelings.
>
> Tonight, Gabe and I are supposed to go to the store and get a bouncy seat, some nursing bras, and a few other things. We planned on leaving her with Gabe's mom, but I can't do it! I don't want to leave her!
>
> Tomorrow, she's supposed to go back to the hospital for her repeat PKU test. I don't want to take her! I don't want to put her in a car seat and drive in a car with her! It scares me to death.
>
> I never want her to leave the house, and I never want to leave her. So I can't leave the house either, I guess. Not ever. *Lord, I really need Your help!*

I don't remember how or when that fear finally subsided. She's obviously been out of the house a time or two in the past seven years. And even spent quite a few nights away from Mommy.

I know you can relate to those crazy fears for your newborn.

Sometimes, your romantic peaceful nights are interrupted by a sudden sense that something is going to happen to your precious baby. In the brightness of the day, you realize that your nighttime fears are irrational, but when they hit in the middle of the night, they are as real as the nose on your face.

What if he stops breathing? What if she spits up and starts choking? What if he needs me, and I don't wake up?

How can you surrender to sleep when your baby is so tiny, so fragile, so helpless, so dependent on you for his every need? How will you survive if something happens to your child? You cry tears of fear, of sorrow, of loss. You imagine the worst, hoping that will somehow prepare you if something horrible ever does happen.

Then morning comes. And all is well. *Thank You, Lord,* you pray. *Help me not to be afraid.*

So many great verses in the Bible offer comfort for nighttime in particular. God knows how much worse things seem in the dark. That's why He calls Himself light.

"I will both lie down in peace, and sleep; for You alone, O LORD, make me dwell in safety" (Psalm 4:8 NKJV).

What a great verse to recite each night before you climb into bed.

Your Greatest Fears

We moms can be a fearful bunch. Nothing is deeper than the bond between a mother and her child, and the very thought of something happening to one of our children is very nearly more than we can bear. As the old saying goes, "The decision to have a child is the decision to forever let your heart walk around outside your body." It's true.

When I asked moms to share their innermost fears, the two I heard over and over and over again were (1) I'm afraid of something happening to my child physically—kidnapping, disease, death—and (2) I'm afraid my child will grow up and choose not to follow Christ.

Some of these answers are heartrending; others will just make you grin. All of them are very real.

I'm sharing them with you not to give you even more reasons to be afraid but because I want you to know that you are not alone in your anxieties and fears. And I'm going to follow up those fears with some incredible promises from God's Word—promises that were of utmost comfort to these same moms when they were feeling afraid.

What are you most anxious or fearful about as a mom?

> "The idea that one day my daughter will have thoughts about me like the ones I had about my mom."

"I'm afraid that I'm going to forget things—special moments, funny moments, feelings."

"I was afraid of everything that was near the baby. Dogs, plants, small objects, dust mites, cancer, car seats, airplanes, swimming pools; it was exhausting. I checked her breathing ten times a night."

"At first it was little things, like how do I go to the grocery store? What do I do with the baby carrier? How do I open the stroller? Now, it's on to bigger things, like will we do a good job? Will he still love us when he's 30?"

"Losing one of my girls. Especially having them kidnapped."

"I really fear that I will fail my children, and they will not grow up to love the Lord."

"That my kids will turn out just like me!"

"Accidents and illnesses—it consumes me some days. Sirens in the distance can paralyze me if I am not sure where everyone is. I really wish that I was not this way. It is a terrible burden and not a great testimony for my faith."

"I don't want my children to have emotional baggage as adults because of me."

"My imperfections and sin coming through and negatively affecting how I train and teach my kids. More than anything, I want them to know Christ and to know how to come to Him with their sin in exchange for grace."

"Them growing up and going to school. Right now I can control all their outside influences. When they go to school, it will be a whole new ball game."

"What if they make bad choices? How do I fill them full of everything good? How do I protect them without being overprotective?"

"Disciplining in public—or in front of my mother-in-law."

"Me being killed in a car wreck and my daughter wondering where her mommy went."

"The thought that one or more of my children might not become a Christian is unbearable to me!"

"My brother is gay, and watching my mom go through that has put fear in me. I never want to walk that road."

"I am nervous about the world and other people being a greater influence on our kids than we are. I would like them to stay small and sheltered longer than is probably healthy for their normal development."

"That when my children move away they won't want to come back."

"I used to worry about SIDS and bathtub drowning. Now I worry that I'm going to wake up tomorrow, and he'll be 16 and won't let me kiss him anymore."

"Not preparing them enough for the battlefield."

"I always feel like something horrible will happen to her that I could have prevented."

"I was afraid the boys would make one little mistake and wind up robbing a convenience store."

"Potty training!"

"That as they reach legal age, they'll run to their biological father instead of clinging to the man that raised them and loved them."

Perfect Love Casts Out Fear

It was 10:00 p.m. My youngest was only a few weeks old. She had been sleeping on a blanket on the living room floor for about three hours. I was ready to hit the hay, so I woke her up to change her diaper, put pajamas on her, nurse her, and put her to bed.

She woke up grinning and cooing and being her adorable self, and for some reason (hormones, exhaustion, Satan), I felt my heart being squeezed to the point of "I can't take this anymore." Her cuteness was just about more than I could bear. I wanted to fly up to heaven and take my little family with me so I never had to worry about something happening to one of them.

It's that whole heart-outside-your-body phenomenon again. Sometimes my heart just aches with love for my little girls. It's a real, physical pain—sometimes a dull throb, other times a sharp stab.

I knew that everything would seem better in the morning. It's amazing how darkness intensifies fear. Just goes to show that Satan is behind it. My fear was real, and I needed some immediate comfort. So I read 1 John 4—promises from God Himself that He loves my babies even more than I do. And that if something ever did happen to one of them, they would be safe in heaven with Him, and He would get me through it somehow, some way.

"There is no fear in love," 1 John 4:18 tells us, "but perfect love drives out fear."

What does that mean? To me, it means that if I really, truly believe that God loves me, if I study His Word and even begin to comprehend the depth of His love for me, I will never be paralyzed or controlled by fear. I will know so deeply that God loves me and wants what's best for me that nothing can move me. God's will is going to prevail. Always. What have I to fear?

It takes a very mature believer to get to that point, and I'm afraid I'm not there yet, but I'm getting closer.

How many times are we told in God's Word not to fear? A ton.

"So do not fear, for I am with you; do not be dismayed, for I am your God. I will strengthen you and help you; I will uphold you with my righteous right hand" (Isaiah 41:10).

"Whoever listens to me will live in safety and be at ease, without fear of harm" (Proverbs 1:33).

"I sought the LORD, and he answered me; he delivered me from all my fears" (Psalm 34:4).

And one of my absolute favorites—"Do not be anxious about anything, but in everything, by prayer and petition, with thanksgiving, present your requests to God. And the peace of God, which transcends all understanding, will guard your hearts and your minds in Christ Jesus" (Philippians 4:6-7).

Dreams for Your Kids

Enough talk about fears—let's talk about hopes and expectations and dreams! What do you dream for your baby? If you're completely honest, what do you hope and wish she will turn out to be someday?

I have all kinds of dreams for my girls—some big, some small. One of them is for all of us to serve together in some ministry capacity in the future. Whether or not that ever happens is up to God. My biggest dream—what I pray for with all of my heart—is that they will love Christ unabashedly and desire to follow Him every moment of their lives.

And if I'm honest, I'll admit that I want them to be strong and beautiful and smart and athletic and successful. To have lots of friends and stay out of trouble. To discover their talents and do something amazing with them. To be well-rounded world travelers, knowledgeable about our universe. To make a difference in the world.

My friend Gail shares similar aspirations with gut-level honesty. "I've been surprised at how much I invest my own hopes and dreams in my children," she says. "I have visions of their future. I desperately want them to be healthy physically, spiritually, and emotionally, to succeed academically and socially, to be positive contributors to society. Should any of that not come to fruition, I don't know how I will handle it."

This is where prayer is so crucial. Carving time out of every busy day to ask for God's blessing on our children.

Another friend has dreams for her little girl as well. "She needs to know she can be anything she wants to be," my friend says. "That with God all things are possible. She is His princess. I dream for her to walk in truth. Where God leads, I pray she follows."

"My dream is that my kids are happy and healthy and enjoy their life," my friend Holly says." I hope to play a role as they walk through their lives, but they will be the directors and I'll be an extra."

"The only real dream I have for my daughter is for her to love and serve the Lord," Nichole says. "Becoming a parent has brought me so much closer in my relationship with Him, and I pray that she will share the same love for Him that I have. I am going to play a critical role in that dream—everything from how I conduct myself in my home to driving us to church on Sunday morning. God has given me this incredible responsibility, and I just can't blow it. I *won't* blow it!"

"I dream of them living happy and fulfilled lives," my friend Kristen says of her two little boys. "I would love for them to one day get married and have children of their own. I dream of having friendships with my children that last forever—deep, healthy, and enriching relationships. I would love to have all of my kids come home when they are older and laugh and reminisce and cherish the good times we are building right now. I pray that they are friends with one another. I would love for my kids to be involved in ministry somehow, but I will support them in whatever the Lord calls them to. I pray they are sensitive to His leading, whatever it may be."

What dreams do you have for your babies? Don't be afraid to dream big. And don't just dream—turn those dreams into prayers! Pray for God's will to be done in their lives, that they will desire nothing more than to follow Christ with their lives.

I know these verses in Jeremiah 29 are quoted a lot, but they're just so beautiful. Most of us are familiar with the New International Version—"'For I know the plans I have for you,' declares the LORD, 'plans to prosper you and not to harm you, plans to give you hope and a future.'"

Let's look at verses 11-14 in The Message for a fresh perspective. Think long and hard about the implications of these words.

"I know what I'm doing. I have it all planned out—plans to take care of you, not abandon you, plans to give you the future you hope for. When you call on me, when you come and pray to me, I'll listen.

When you come looking for me, you'll find me. Yes, when you get serious about finding me and want it more than anything else, I'll make sure you won't be disappointed."

God will listen to our prayers for our children. He wants to bless them, and I'm not talking about money, but about the best kinds of blessings God has to give.

When we seek God first, He promises that everything else we need—deliverance from fear, hope for the future—will be given to us as well (Matthew 6:33).

Crucified with Christ

I strongly feel led to add a PS of sorts to the end of this chapter. As much as I want my children to know happiness and health, safety and success, most of all I want them to be passionate about Jesus Christ and sharing the message of the cross with the world.

And like it or not, this often comes with a hefty price tag. If my daughters have to endure ridicule, persecution, or even physical danger, may that pale in comparison to loving Christ and living for Him.

I pray that God will mold my heart in such a way that my one overpowering desire for my babies is that Christ be glorified in their lives—regardless of the cost.

It's All
Relative

5

From Hubby to Daddy

Do you remember being engaged and dreaming about the day you'd finally be married? Did you envision a romantic, blissful cuddle fest with your new hubby? Were you picturing him coming home from work, a dozen roses in tow, thrilled down to his toenails to be reuniting with you after eight long hours apart?

Did you dream about long-drawn-out heart-to-heart chats, delightful shared shopping experiences, leisurely walks around the neighborhood hand-in-hand, nights of slow, delicious lovemaking?

You thought the cares of life would just all magically fall away, didn't you? After all, you're *married* now. And marriage is the end all, be all, ultimate picture of contentment.

Except it's not.

Slowly but surely, you realized that your husband is human. That he sometimes just wants to scratch himself and watch a football game (or six) in peace. That he'd rather grunt than talk, he'd rather hunt than shop, and he'd rather save for retirement (or a new toy) than buy expensive flowers.

If you're smart, you'll let go of some of those lofty expectations you once held, and you'll work on making a good marriage out of the raw materials you have on hand. And if you open your eyes and look around (and find some friends who are honest), you'll see that this is what *real* marriage is like.

If you take the time and make the effort, you can have a marriage that may look a lot different from the marriage of your dreams but be more fulfilling than you could have imagined.

You settle in, on your way to contentment, and then it happens. The baby bug hits, you get pregnant, and those pesky expectations raise their little heads once more.

He'll Be the Best Daddy Ever!

You start doing that daydreaming thing again. But this time, the two cuddling on the couch are your hubby and your brand-new baby. But wait, we're getting ahead of ourselves.

Your first dreamy visions include that tiny egg and itty-bitty sperm colliding in a blast of ecstasy. Then you fast-forward a couple weeks to your positive pregnancy test. You dream of all the ways you might tell him your happy news. You picture him crying tears of joy and looking at you with such love and admiration in his eyes. You see him squealing with excitement and telling everyone he meets that he's about to be a daddy.

Then you picture him protectively accompanying you to every prenatal appointment, spending hours each evening rubbing your feet and stroking your belly. Then the romance of your water breaking, rushing to the hospital, and giving birth to your first child. You'll be his hero for bringing his child safely into the world.

Then comes that daddy-baby bonding time on the couch. He'll offer to do baby duty while you get some much-needed rest. Football, video games, and deer season will fade into the background. He won't be able to get enough of his precious child. He was born to be a daddy. Nothing else matters.

And on and on and on...

What *Really* Happens

I'll be honest with you. Some men *do* take to their new daddy role like it's their destiny. They actually do many of those things you fantasized your husband would.

But for many, many other husbands, being a father is like being a fish out of water. It makes him uncomfortable. He just doesn't have that parenting instinct. He'd rather watch the game than watch the baby lie in his bassinet (if you can believe that!). He finds the loss of his freedom quite disconcerting. His wife's affections have been stolen away by a very small, boring, sometimes very loud little creature. He'd like some attention back. And man, does he miss the sex!

If your marriage is normal and you're normal, you've probably found yourself disappointed in your husband as a father at least once since you conceived this child. Maybe even countless times.

"It was frustrating trying to get my husband excited about my pregnancy," one woman said. "He didn't want to feel the baby move very often, and it was a struggle for him to talk about the baby."

I remember being annoyed that Gabe just wasn't as consumed with my pregnancy as I was. Nor did he seem as taken with our newborn daughter. *What's his deal?* I thought. He wasn't overly eager to take on any of the routine parenting tasks. He didn't volunteer his help—I had to ask. And he was deathly afraid of being left alone with her.

"My husband had a really difficult time," says another woman, "and it was a challenge to help him through the transition to fatherhood as well as take care of a baby. I felt as if I was forced to balance a fussy baby and a fussy husband both at once!"

"We were only married six months before getting pregnant," one friend told me, "so we had a lot that was never accomplished or solidified before we added a child. I think the loss of freedom was especially hard on my husband."

"I thought my husband would adjust to parenting as easily as I did," says one woman. "It probably took a few years for his relationship with our children to be as strong as mine."

I'm not trying to burst your bubble. If you've read my previous books, you know that I just like keeping things real. You know that I think a husband is a gift from God and that marriage, sex, and shared parenthood are some of life's most incredible blessings. Some of these ooey-gooey daydreams of yours will actually play out (at times) in real life!

I'm just saying we don't live in a fairy tale, and when our expectations are crazy-lofty, we aren't being fair to our husbands. For the most part, they are good men doing the best they can. We need to pray for them, shower them with grace, and do away with the selfishness. (If they have bigger-than-normal issues, we'll have to kick our prayers into overdrive and maybe get some outside help.)

Our disappointment in hubby-as-daddy often stems from one of two things:

1. We're expecting them to act more like mothers, but they are fathers. In other words, we were created to be nurturers. Our husbands are gifted in other ways. Their love for our children is going to be different from ours, plain and simple.

2. We've completely taken off our wife hat, tossed it carelessly in the messy coat closet, and surgically attached the mommy hat to our heads. And when we elevate our baby's needs above our husband's, when we can't seem to be a wife and mommy at the same time, our marriage is going to suffer. As I've said before, a happy hubby is a better daddy.

Fifty-Fifty?

Before I talk about our marriages and how motherhood affects them, I'd like to get a little housekeeping out of the way. Actually, I'd like to talk about the division of household chores and baby duty. Who does what? And how do you decide what's fair? Does such a thing even exist?

"The hardest times were when all three kids were little and someone always needed something," Sandi B. says. "We got into a habit of keeping score of who had the most free time or who ate the last hot meal while the other walked the baby. We had many power struggles before we finally figured out what worked for us."

So how much dirty work (childcare and housekeeping) should

hubby have to do? Oh, the age-old question. The answer used to be obvious: none. Dad goes to work, comes home, and relaxes. Mom stays home all day, takes care of the kids and the house. No biggie.

Then we women got all liberated and stuff. Instead of Mom being pregnant, *we're* pregnant. Instead of Dad waiting outside the delivery room, he coaches and catches babies and cuts umbilical cords. Instead of Mom staying home, more often than not, she works.

So when Mom and Dad are both at home in the evenings and on weekends, who changes the diapers and feeds the baby? Who's got bath duty? Who takes care of the house? The laundry? The cooking?

Oh, this is not really a debate I enjoy. Most of you aren't going to like my opinion.

I tend to take a pretty traditional stance on childcare and housework. I do the bulk of it. I've always looked at diaper changing, feeding, bathing, and dressing babies as my responsibility. (Not that I always do it joyfully, mind you.) Gabe helps out when he gets the urge (which is *much* more often than it used to be) or when I specifically ask him to give me a hand.

I've always wanted to be a mom. Gabe didn't grow up counting down the days until fatherhood. Since I was the one who wanted the babies so badly, I feel as if taking care of them is my job. I want Gabe to look at our kids as a joy and a blessing, not a burden. One of the ways I can help improve his attitude toward them is to handle most of the work involved.

Of course, this can lead to exhaustion, which then leads to a bad attitude on my part, so it can get a little tricky.

Melissa can relate. "It's easy for me to just do things without giving Ed the chance," she says. "At times though, this makes him feel left out and me feel wiped out."

Where's the best balance? Who knows?

The way I see it, Gabe works eight hours a day in an office. I don't. He's tired. I'm not. (Ha! Just checking to see if you were paying attention.) If I worked outside the home, I might view things differently. Or maybe I wouldn't.

Some dads love newborns and eagerly change diapers, do late-night feedings, and give sponge baths. Gabe's not opposed to babies, but he feels more comfortable with little people who can walk and talk.

As the girls got older, Gabe found his daddy niche and began playing with them more, taking them out on dates, wrestling with them and letting them jump on him, and going for walks and bike rides.

And by the time little Nina arrived, he felt much more at ease in the daddy-baby relationship. They've been buds for a long time now, and she's not even two.

Mr. Mom

Gabe got better and better with each new child—gotta love a man who gets better with age—but one friend was bummed to discover that the opposite seemed true with her husband.

"My husband was completely different with number one than he is with number two," she said. "With our first, he would take her all the time when she was screaming. He'd get up in the middle of the night to let me get some sleep. He actually liked the project of finding out what was wrong with her.

"This time, I practically have to beg to get him to get up at night when I'm at my wit's end. He's much less interested in the newborn-ness of it all. I've even accused him of not liking the baby. He said that wasn't true. He just doesn't know what to do to calm him and get him back to sleep, so it's much more efficient if I do it. It's frustrating when he doesn't even try to figure it out. It is getting better, though."

"I sometimes feel like I'm doing everything by myself," another friend said. "which is part of being a full-time stay-at-home mom, I think. My husband couldn't possibly do as much as I do because that's all I do! I think he sometimes struggles with proving to others (and me) that he can take care of a baby. He was completely new to this when our daughter was born. The first diaper he ever changed was one at the hospital."

Megan's husband changed lots of diapers in the hospital. "My husband is a terrific daddy," she says. "He jumped right in from the moment our son was born. In fact, I'm not sure I ever changed a diaper in the hospital. He is always looking to give 100 percent. Sometimes it is difficult for me when he has to be out of town for a few days or when he is needed at the church and I am home with the little guy by myself. I do get frustrated when the time that my husband has spent with our son is significantly less than the time that I have spent with him. But most of the time, these things are not in my husband's control."

"It is difficult at the end of the day when I am very ready for my husband to take over the parent role," says one woman, "as I have been meeting every need all day. I am trying to be a good wife and have a meal prepared and the house picked up, and the baby still wants me to hold him. I'm tired, and I feel like my husband thinks I was sitting around all day rather than getting things accomplished. But he's tired from working all day as well and needs time to relax. I wish he would just step up and help out on his own."

One solution that worked well for a friend of mine was just to do the obvious—have twins.

"Having two at once actually gave us an advantage," Gail says. "It never felt like I was siding with a kid, leaving my husband out. He was rocking a baby at the same time I was. We went into the parenting as a partnership. He got up every night with me, diapering and soothing one twin while I was nursing the other one. That idea of sharing the load lent an unusual camaraderie to our approach to parenting."

What Should We Expect?

Don't run out and have twins just to save yourself the trouble of divvying up diaper duty. I'm sure that having two at one time has its share of challenges (ya think?).

For the other 97 percent of us, I think honesty tempered with kindness is the best approach.

Men have this amazing ability to feign ignorance (or maybe they honestly don't know) when their assistance might be requested, and they'd much rather just continue in their vegetative state (in the recliner, computer chair, or bed).

I've found that the method that works best for us is for me to ask kindly, state exactly what I'd like to be done, and never lay on a guilt trip.

"Gabe, I need to take a shower. Could you please watch the baby for 15 minutes? Thank you."

I cringe when I hear wives bossing their husbands around concerning baby duty, especially in front of other people. You're at a family reunion, and you hear (*everybody* hears), "John, can I get a little help here? Your son needs changed. His diaper is sagging out of his shorts. I've got my hands full, and you're standing around doing nothing. It sure would be nice if you'd pay attention to *your* child for once."

Our men would get the third degree (and no sex for two months) if they talked that way to us.

I think it's highly unfair to expect your husband to go from hubby-lover to mother's helper overnight. He married a wife, and they had all kinds of fun. Now he's married to a mother, and his only pleasures in life are helping her with her parenting tasks.

What if your husband brought home an expensive sports car (or two!) and told you, "Honey, I need you to work extra hours at the office to pay the bills and keep my cars looking spiffy. No more dinners out, shopping sprees, or chats with girlfriends over coffee. From now on, when you come home from work, I'm going to need you to wash, wax, and vacuum our cars. I'll be worn out from spending all day with them, and they're going to need some lovin' from you while I get a break."

Ha! Can you imagine?

Communicate with your husband what it is that you'd like. He can't read your mind or anticipate your desires. He really can't. Don't demand. Share your ideas. Ask him if he thinks that's fair. If not, why not?

Make a plan you can both live with.

Transition from Wife to Mommy

If you're struggling with the jump from wife to mommy, climb in the boat with the rest of us! The thing that makes it so hard is that you aren't really making a jump at all. You're straddling two cliffs—the wife cliff and the mommy cliff. You're trying to be both without pulling a groin muscle or plunging into the ravine below.

"Our transition was a little rocky," Lindsey says. "My husband was a wonderful support, but I had to figure out this whole mommy thing before I could turn my attention back to him. It took a while to find a balance, which I still struggle with on certain days. Especially the days when they all need me at the same time."

"The transition from wife to mommy was a bit stressful at first," Mindy says. "I felt pulled in a lot of different directions and didn't feel I was doing either justice. Luckily, my husband has always been a huge help and because we are a team, things smoothed themselves out."

"It was tricky," one woman told me. "It was easy for me to just move from wife to mommy, but difficult for me to learn how to maintain the wife component. It probably took a good nine months for me to get the hang of being both wife and mommy. Even now, after nearly six years of being a mommy, it is still easy for me to lapse more into mommy mode."

"Being a mom came very naturally to me," my friend Rachael says. "Changing diapers, nursing, understanding the baby's cries—I got all that. The hard part for me was figuring how to make my husband still feel like he was a priority to me—and meet my baby's needs at the same time."

"It put a huge strain on our marriage!" one woman told me. "A pastor once told me that with each child, your chances of your marriage surviving get less and less."

"We have always stressed the importance of my role as wife first, mommy second," Gail says. "I don't think I lost my love, my passion, my commitment to my husband. I just added some other duties. Many, many, many other duties."

Gail hit it on the nose. Wife first, mommy second. It's not until after we're both that we realize just how tough it is to keep them in that order.

"Being a mom comes easier to me than being a wife does," one woman said. "I'm more selfish when it comes to having to take care of my husband than I am with my daughter. It's easier to be a selfless mommy than a selfless wife."

"I felt torn a lot between my son and my husband," one friend told me. "I wanted to be there and care for them both, but the baby took up so much energy that I struggled to find time for my husband."

"The two transitions were so close together that they really were blurred," says Claudia. "Looking back, I realize that most of the 'problems' in our marriage were more related to the marriage transition than having a baby."

Ideally, I think a marriage needs a little bit of time to grow before the kiddos come along. But, if not, you'll just grow together as you go, which can also be pretty cool. That's what my friend Cherith and her husband did with their conceived-right-after-the-wedding baby.

"I think the wife-to-mommy transition came pretty naturally to me," she says, "but maybe that was because I had only been a wife for about ten months and there weren't really any dead-set routines that we had to give up."

"When you marry, you have to get rid of selfishness, and realize it's not just me, myself, and I anymore," one woman said. "When you become a mom, it hits you like a ton of bricks!"

"I felt so overwhelmed and emotional," one friend told me, "that trying to make intimate time with my husband a priority felt almost scary. I was afraid I'd cry through the whole thing because I was still adjusting to everything and was tired to the point of not really being all there."

"I went into the hospital in labor wearing my pretty bra and thong underwear," one woman told me. "I left the hospital in a nursing bra and granny panties."

That about sums it up right there, folks.

Making Hubby a Priority

When I asked women to tell me how motherhood has affected

their marriage, I wasn't surprised to find that almost all of them mentioned having to find time for their marriage or make a conscious effort to meet their husbands' needs (or some other variation of the same theme).

Now, let's try to look at this from our husbands' perspectives. How would you like it if he told you he'd try to squeeze you in between golf games or he had to force himself to sit down and have a chat with you? What if you were relegated to an item on his to-do list?

No one wants to feel like a duty or an obligation. We want to feel loved and cherished and desired.

So do our husbands.

Now, here's the deal. When your kids are little, making time for your husband is going to take a huge effort. There's no way around it. The key is making time for him without letting on that it takes that much effort.

I'm not talking about deception. I'm talking about being unselfish and having a good attitude—not playing martyr-wife. I'm talking about asking God to give you strength from His divine supply because yours has been all used up with late-night feedings, 12 diaper changes a day, keeping dirty dishes from o'ertaking your kitchen counters, and…you get the point.

Here are some thoughts from women who want to be good wives. Some of them are getting a handle on it; some of them have a way to go. Some of them have some helpful tips for the rest of us. If nothing else, I hope you'll be encouraged by their honesty. I asked them, how has motherhood affected your marriage?

"At first I was so focused on being a good mother that I became a lousy wife," Claudia admits. "I would expend all my energy on our children and have nothing left for my husband. It took a long time before I was willing to admit this and deal with it. I was fortunate to have a very patient, committed, and loving husband who was willing to wait on me!"

"When the kids are young and so needy, it is hard to strike a correct balance," says my friend Krista. "You are zapped of all energy by the end of the day, and the last thing you want to do is meet somebody else's needs. Almost daily, I have to remind myself of the order of my roles. Christ follower first, wife second, mother third."

"It has required more effort to stay connected with my husband," says my friend Joanne. "At the end of the day, I'm tired. I have to remember to fill him in on what's going on with me and to ask him about what's going on with him."

"With our first child, it deepened our respect and our love for one another," says one woman, "that we actually created this child together. With our second child, things were much different. My husband really felt cheated on time—like I was always giving to one of the kids and there was nothing left over for him."

"One word...*sex!*" says Sara. "It's hard to have a lot when little ones are nursing around the clock or have invaded your bed. But when we could sneak it in, it was exciting, because we never knew how much time we had!"

"A lot less sex," says one woman. "My husband often feels neglected because our son needed so much of my attention. I have had to make a conscious effort to make him feel important."

"My husband and I have to make time for each other," another woman says, "and consciously make the decision not to let ourselves become business partners who are raising a child instead of lovers and friends."

"It's very hard to let down the curtains of mommy-hood and just be a wife," says Anne Marie. "It's very hard to feel sexy and focus on putting my husband before my kids."

"It has been stressful," says my friend Jamie. "I feel like my husband and I have to work even harder than before to find time for one another. When we don't, it shows."

"When my husband and I haven't taken time for us as a couple" says one woman, "I feel very distant from him—not like a wife, more like a maid."

"My attention at times is directed more at children than at my spouse," says one friend. "I stay home with our children, and they can easily become my life. I have to try to be careful and balance myself."

"I have had to do some attitude checks on myself," Gail says. "Am I keeping my relationship to my husband as important as I should? Am I meeting his needs? Am I keeping a perspective on what the kids' actual needs are? Watching for signs of child-centered thoughts has helped us keep our marriage healthy."

We could all stand to do a daily attitude check, couldn't we? And check the stinky ones at the door!

Better After Baby

Ready for some marital encouragement? Yes, babies can throw your marriage for a loop, but when you work together through something as tough as parenthood, you can forge one pretty strong bond.

Without any prompting, some wonderful women shared some words of inspiration to keep fighting for our marriages to the very end. The two of you are so worth it.

"Parenthood has strengthened my marriage in many ways," Lindsey says. "I have a new appreciation and love for my husband. Seeing him with my girls makes me that much more attracted to him."

"It has made us stronger," Mindy says. "Yes, there is less alone time, but we always laugh when we do have a date night because we feel like something is missing. We always wondered what we did with our time before Ella was born. Things that seemed so important before (like doing your hair and makeup) don't really matter as much."

"It has both challenged and enhanced it," one woman said. "We've grown together a lot by parenting—both messing up and succeeding."

"It has intensified my love for my spouse," says my friend Holly. "It's made me appreciate him in more ways than I can even verbalize."

"It's really what has kept us together during the hard times," says Molly. "Our undying dedication to raising our daughter in a godly home has sealed our commitment to each other."

"Now, with two kids, parenthood seems to make us much more of a team," says Kristen. "We feel unified and dependent on one another to get through this crazy time."

"Parenthood has drawn my husband and me together more closely than we ever would have imagined," says my friend Camille. "It is the hardest and most rewarding thing we have ever done as a team."

Go to Great Lengths

"We're keeping in mind that the children will eventually be adults," says Michelle, "and we'll still have each other. We go to great lengths to prevent waking up in 20 years as strangers."

As impossible as it seems, a day will come when your last baby walks down the aisle and you and hubby are left alone in an empty nest. If you wait until then to fortify that nest, it will be too late. It's gonna crumble.

The time is now, friend. Even if your first baby is just days old. What can you do *right now* to show your hubby some lovin'? To remind yourself why you married him? To keep those flames of love burning even in the midst of mommy-hood?

It's okay to start small, but start! You know your hubby (at least you used to!). You know what would make him smile. When in doubt, sex is a pretty universal love-expression (*Is That All He Thinks About?* is a fun read to get that party started!).

Figure out his love language. Learn what makes him tick. Carve out some time for him. Ask God for time and energy where none exist. Spend feeding moments and diaper moments and laundry moments in prayer.

Last year, on my husband's thirtieth birthday, I wrote him a little poem on my blog in honor of the man he has become. And wow, has he come a long way in our ten years of marriage! I'm obviously no poet, but it's the thought that counts.

I think he liked it, even if poetry was a distant fourth on his birthday wish list (after sex, computer software, and all-you-can-eat Mongolian BBQ).

My Hubby, My Friend

G God is first in my husband's life. The more time that goes by, the more he wants to know who God is and grow closer and closer to Him. Watching him grow drives me to grow too.

A As attractive as the day we met. The girl campers all had a crush on my future hubby, the camp counselor, and called him "Gabe the Babe." The name still applies today. Even more so actually.

B Best daddy three little girls could ever, ever want. They adore him. Their eyes light up when he walks in the door from work. They roar with laughter when he plays with them and tickles them. He invents games and stories and teaches them life lessons they'll remember forever. They are blessed beyond measure.

R Real and honest, a man of integrity. What you see is what you get. No games, no dishonesty. He's the real deal, and I trust him with every ounce of me.

I In love with his wife *unconditionally* after all this time and all the grief she's put him through. He loves her mind, her body, her spirit—unexplainable, but he makes it beautifully obvious.

E Ever learning, ever growing, he is fascinated by the world around him. He wants to know more and more, never content with the knowledge and skills he possesses today. Always has something interesting to discuss, and his wife finds this very attractive.

L Life wouldn't be life without him in it. I need him. *We* need him. He is such a vital part of us. He's why I wake up in the morning.

Stand by Your Man

I know that you may not have a husband to do this parenting thing with, and my heart goes out to you. Hang in there, you precious single mom! God knows the desires of your heart, and He alone knows what you need most in life. He will never leave you, He will never forsake you, and He will be faithful to provide for your every need.

If you are married, listen up. Whatever it takes, you want to nurture this marriage of yours! I leave you with some of Paul's words. "Trust steadily in God, hope unswervingly, love extravagantly. And the best of the three is love. Go after a life of love as if your life depended on it—because it does" (1 Corinthians 13:13–14:1 MSG).

Thank God for that hubby He gave you, and love him as if your life depended on it!

6

The Grandparent Factor

You take a tentative step toward the counter. You look up at the menu.

"May I take your order?" the young man says.

You hesitate. "Uh, could I have a moment please?"

"Sure. Take your time." The words suggest patience beyond his years. His tone and rolled eyes scream sarcastic adolescent.

Silence ensues. He rolls his eyes again.

"Okay, I think I'm ready."

"Okay..."

"Yeah," you say. "Right. Um, I'll take a...I'll take a husband...an order of kids on the side..."

You pause.

"Will that be all?"

"Um, yeah. I mean, no! One more thing. Um, could you hold the in-laws, please?"

If only life were that easy.

Oh, Sweet In-Laws

I've said before that sex can't be bad because God created it before the fall. The same cannot be said, however, for in-laws. They're an entirely different story. They didn't come on the scene until the third generation of humans.

And don't ask me to explain *that*. God made a man and woman—Adam and Eve. They obviously didn't have a mother-in-law or father-in-law. And then their kids evidently grew up and started marrying each other. So that second generation had Mom and Dad for in-laws.

But I digress. You live in the twenty-first century. And if you're married, you more than likely have in-laws.

My cousin Kelly once asked me (semiseriously), "When I meet my future husband, is it wrong to hope all his relatives are dead?"

I can see the ad now. "Wanted: Tall, dark, handsome man. Age 25–30. Please, no living kin."

Just last year, I had plans to write an entire book on in-laws until the fine folks in the world of publishing regretfully informed me it wouldn't sell. Seems that women want to work on their marriages and their mothering. They'd even like to see improvement in their spiritual lives and in their homes. But making an effort to get along better with their in-laws? Not so much.

Whether we want to talk about them or not, you can only avoid the in-laws for so long. And when children enter the picture, the game suddenly gets more complicated.

When Grandparents Are Born

Times sure have changed, haven't they? And this becomes quite apparent when you become a parent and your own parental units (and your husband's) remind you of the fact.

"That's not the way *we* did it."

"Back when *you* were growing up, it was unheard of to..."

"This has worked for hundreds of years. I don't know why young parents think they need to change things now."

Depending on your personality, you may crave the help and advice your mom and mother-in-law are more than willing to give. Or that independent spirit of yours may balk every time you see that look in their eyes—the look that says they disapprove, however mildly, of the way you're mothering your child.

A wise grandma will stay out of your way, offer up lots of prayers on your (and her grandchild's!) behalf, and give advice only when specifically asked for it. But that can't be an easy thing to do. Especially when she's had years and years of experience that you lack.

You know what it's like watching a newbie struggle with something you've mastered over time. Whether it's knitting or mountain biking, juggling or cake decorating, if you know how it's done, and you see someone doing it wrong, it's hard to bite your tongue.

So go easy on Grandma. And do your best to make sure you and hubby are a team. Some new moms are going to struggle with this more than others. Every family dynamic is different. We're all imperfect people trying to live together as extended families in this crazy world. A bit of love and grace go a long way in smoothing things over and surviving family get-togethers or even daily life—depending on how close you live to your in-laws.

Different Philosophies

Most moms of grown kids are pretty confident that the way they raised their babies was best. And if they're feeling insecure about it, they usually try to justify it or convince others it was best anyway.

Your parenting choices are unique—based on many factors. How your mom and dad raised you (and whether or not you liked it), what you've read, what you've seen, what you believe.

So what do you do when you've made a choice and your parents and in-laws aren't sure it was the best one?

One friend of mine decided to use a certain child-rearing method with her son and says her mother-in-law just didn't get it.

"At first it was hard because I didn't know how to communicate our philosophy without offending her," my friend told me. "She kept telling me she rocked my husband for two hours each night. And I felt very nervous about telling her we weren't planning on rocking our baby to sleep."

One friend breast-fed her baby boy and chose to stay home with him instead of returning to work. "My husband and I decided this was best for us," she says. "My mother-in-law did the opposite, and she says she thinks we judge her because of that."

One woman had nothing but praise for her in-laws but was continually frustrated by her own parents. "I really hate sending my kids over there for the day," she says. "Whatever they ask for is what they eat—candy, cereal, popcorn—and it usually ends up being their supper. My parents don't respect our wishes on anything we ask. They think they're the experts just because they had kids before we did."

"We discipline our children," one woman says, "and my father-in-law thinks that kids should be able to express themselves freely. I think we have just agreed to disagree."

Be Careful with Expectations

Just as we expect that marriage will be one big make-out fest on a rug in front of the fireplace, and life with a newborn means days filled with scents of baby powder and roses, we set some pretty high expectations for our children's grandparents as well.

We picture the loving, doting grandma and grandpa who drop everything for their grandchild, carry huge photo albums everywhere they go, and beg to babysit while you go out with your husband.

This happens for some people, sure, but not all. Some grandparents just don't measure up to your ideal. Maybe they're too busy to spend time with your kids. Maybe they enjoy their freedom too much to want kids around all the time. Maybe your parents and in-laws fight over your kids. Maybe you see favoritism being shown to your baby's cousins. Maybe you have such differences of opinion on raising children that fights ensue every time you're together.

Maybe it's a good thing I didn't write that in-law book because the more I think about it, how in the world do we ever figure this thing out?

"Neither set of parents are as affectionate with our kids as I had hoped," said one friend. "When they're around my kids, they're still too busy doing stuff to take the time to sit down and hold or play with them."

One woman expected her in-laws to love her daughter as much as her own parents do, and she was quite disappointed. "His mom and stepdad visited once to see our daughter when she was born (three months ago). His dad and step-mom have never seen her; they just don't seem anxious to meet her. It boggles my mind because my parents couldn't stand being a mere 45-minute drive away; they moved to the neighborhood! They have us over for dinner virtually every other night, and they swoon over our daughter."

I do know one thing—every story has two sides. This in-law thing is a two-way street. And I know something else. We women (especially we mommy-hormonal ones) have a tendency to see things the way we want to see them. Come on, admit it.

I'm not saying you're to blame for a rough relationship with your child's grandparents. All I'm asking is that you take an honest look at what's going on and ask God if there's any step *you* could take—forget about the other guy for a minute—toward making the relationship a little bit better tomorrow than it is today.

Where's the Love?

Being a mom for the first time (or the second, third, fourth) and feeling like you don't have the support of your parents or in-laws is difficult. Maybe you've misjudged their motives. Maybe you're being unfair. Maybe you're imagining things.

Or maybe it's more fact than fiction. There's just not a whole lotta love comin' your way from the kinfolk.

I'm so thankful for a mom and mom-in-law who constantly praise me for being a good mommy. And I have a feeling that when I'm not so hot at something I'm doing, it just ends up being a nice conversation between them and God, and I don't ever know about it.

Not everyone is so fortunate.

"My parents love our daughter like crazy," one friend said, "but they give a lot of advice and struggle with letting us be the parents."

Another friend says that even though her in-laws aren't very hands-on with their grandkids, "my mother-in-law sure does have a lot of advice about how we should be raising them."

One dear friend loves her parents and her in-laws but wishes that both of them would be a little more "encouraging of our parenting. We are doing our best to raise our kids to be well-rounded, Christ-centered people. It's hard, and sometimes you just want to hear them say that you are doing a good job."

Even if words of affirmation aren't our primary love language, they do our hearts good. So what do we do when we're not getting them?

Sometimes prayer is the best answer. Pray that God would speak to the grandparents' hearts and burden them to ease up on the advice and criticism and be a little freer with the praise.

Some people just aren't good at praise and compliments. They've never been ones to speak affirmingly to others. They feel awkward saying things like, "I think you're doing a really good job raising Johnny."

Some don't even *think* to say it. When they do notice something positive, it doesn't cross their minds to actually verbalize it.

And sadly, some people just don't really notice the positive in life at any level. It's all negativity all the time.

Pray that someday they'll appreciate you and that they'll even let you know it a time or two. And if they never do, pray that God will help you find your worth and acceptance through Christ, not through your parents and in-laws.

If you think communicating your feelings to them directly would help, pray for wisdom and then take the plunge.

"You know, Mom (Mom-in-Law), all you ever do is harp on me! You never have anything nice to say! Would it kill you to say something affirming? You think I'm a lousy mom, and nothing I do will ever be good enough for you!"

Okay, surely we can think of a better way to word that.

How about this? "You know, Mom (Mom-in-Law), I really want to do this parenting thing right, and I'm doing the best I can. I would love to hear some words of encouragement from you. It always makes me feel so good when I know you approve of something I've done. I want you to be proud of me."

Some grandparents will just take more prayer than others.

Like this one. "My mother-in-law, I think, would like to be the mother of my child," says a friend. "She thinks I do a lot wrong, but I expected that. When we first called to tell her we were having a baby, she responded with, 'How did *that* happen?'"

How did it happen indeed.

Kudos for Grandparents

Lots of grandparents have nailed this thing and deserve all the praise we can lavish on them. Even the ones who are still working on it deserve a pat on the back!

Jennifer F. says her mother-in-law "is a saint when it comes to censoring her opinions on my child rearing. She expressed some concern when I stopped breast-feeding and called back within ten minutes of her well-meaning comment, apologizing and telling me that I knew what was best for my baby and me."

Now, that's an encouraging story. Jenn says she understands her mother-in-law much better now than she did before having children. "She and my father-in-law are great encouragers and affirmers of our parenting."

"My in-laws are great," says Jessica P. "It has been neat to hear them express to us that we don't need to raise our children like anyone else. They don't have a mold we need to fit into. They never give unsolicited advice and allow us to be the parents. They love our daughter endlessly."

Jessica's sister Tracie feels the same way about her own in-laws. "They love our son to death," she says. "I'm very happy because I was afraid my mother-in-law would be full of advice for me, but she really holds herself back."

"My in-laws are absolutely wonderful with our kids," says one friend. "They make sure the kids have whole meals and good bedtimes and respect what we say. There really isn't anything to tell them because we know our kids are going to be completely taken care of."

"My father-in-law is the greatest grandpa," says Krystal. "He spends time with the kids, plays with them, and encourages them. He gets to know the kids, and they absolutely love him."

"My in-laws love their grandkids like nobody else," Rachael says. "Our kids are their pride and joy."

And like I said, it's a two-way street. Are *you* taking the time to pat *them* on the back for a job well done? Do you thank them for loving your kiddos? Do you let them know verbally that you recognize their efforts and you appreciate what they do for your babies?

You're never too old to enjoy a genuine compliment—especially coming from your own grown child.

When Grandparents Complement, Not Compete

Gabe and I are blessed when it comes to our extended families. The differences between our parents used to be a source of contention between us. But now that we have kids, we couldn't be more thankful for our parents' unique personalities and ways of life.

Gabe's mom paints their toenails and jumps on the trampoline with them. My mom reads to them and plays board games and card games with them. Both of them are great for taking walks, talking about important stuff, and pushing on swings.

Papaw Rock does Gator rides and horse rides, and Papaw Ron does lawn tractor rides and gives horsy rides on his back! They both live out in the middle of nowhere and like to burn things like trash or marshmallows.

Whatever our girls are in the mood for, they have a grandma or grandpa who fits the bill!

A friend of mine is in the same situation. "My in-laws are good grandparents. They are fun and do lots of activities with them. My parents are also good grandparents. They don't do as many activities, but they play games. They teach them about the Bible and God, and my kids just love it. My kids really love to be at both sets of grandparents' houses but for different reasons."

Gabe and I have made a conscious effort to encourage our girls to love both sets of grandparents equally. And they do!

You might be tempted to tip the scales in your own parents' direction—whether it's by subtle jabs against your in-laws or by only talking about how great your own parents are. Fight the urge. Don't do it.

Some households can't give both (or more!) sets of grandparents equal billing, but do what you can. Grandmas and grandpas are a gift to your little ones, and you want to make sure you do your part to make the relationships healthy and fun.

Grandparents or Babysitters?

I've got a question for you—how often do you call your mother-in-law? Every time you need a babysitter? I raise my hand as a guilty party on this one. Gabe's mom and I have a great relationship, and she loves my girls to death, but I'm sure that every once in a while she thinks, *Wow, it sure would be nice to be loved for who I am and not just as a glorified babysitter.*

It works both ways. A lot of moms in my survey commented that they feel as if they all but disappeared once their kids were born. "My parents don't even see me anymore when we walk in the door. It's all about the baby!"

And some grandparents are probably thinking, "My kids don't even care about me as a person anymore. It's all about whether or not I'm free to babysit so they can go out without the kids!"

"My in-laws are supportive," one woman told me, "but not very helpful. They have no interest in spending time with our kids unless we are there. They are definitely not babysitters."

I can see both sides to this. I try to picture what this will look like when I become a grandma. I don't think I'll want to be "used" either. Do I want Livi and Ava and Nina to just drop their kids off and run—and not give two hoots about me, the woman who invested her life in raising them?

"My mother-in-law loves her grandkids," said one woman, "but she really craves adult interaction more. You won't see her get down and play with them or take much interest in their interests. She's more about herself than about them (or anyone else). It's like they are cute decorations to have around, but she doesn't want them to get in the way of the adult interaction. She never babysits them or takes them on outings or anything like that."

"My parents refuse to babysit the kids," one woman told me. "When we visit, my parents don't pay any attention to them. They won't know my kids as they get older because they don't take the time to get to know them."

One woman said her in-laws are good grandparents but don't make an effort to see the kids very often, despite living just a few miles away. "Yet now my mother-in-law is getting jealous because my 18-month-old daughter favors my mother over her."

One woman says her mother-in-law is great but that she thinks her own parents just don't like kids. "They aren't comfortable around them and expect them to be perfect. They only babysat the oldest as a baby one night, and they have never spent an evening alone with a kid since then. As far as I know, nothing even went wrong. They like to hear about them from time to time, and they pray for them and get them little gifts here and there. It's a very superficial relationship."

That makes my heart a little sad.

Make sure you're being fair in your assessment of "uninterested" grandparents. Some do really seem to be selfish. Retirement means sipping cocktails and collecting seashells—who has time for little rugrats?

But some might just be feeling used, taken for granted, taken advantage of. Again, put yourself in their shoes. You put nearly two decades of your life into raising your children, and then all they care about is, "Are you free to watch Junior for the weekend?"

Show your parents and in-laws that you care about them as people, that you're interested in what's going on in their lives, that you want to spend time with them. It might make a huge difference.

Making Grandma Feel Important

Is your relationship with your mother-in-law strained? Did you find yourself hoping that having a baby might bring you closer together? Has it worked?

One friend shared a secret with me that I found to be ingenious. Her mother-in-law dotes on her grandchildren and their father (her son), but she isn't overly fond of her daughter-in-law.

"Just to give you an idea of what our relationship is like," she says, "If we make a family decision she doesn't like, and I'm the one who tells her about it, she has a big hissy fit. But if my husband shares the same decision with his mom, she sends us off with a big smile and a covered dish!"

This funny friend of mine says she gives her mother-in-law "special missions." She'll tell her something that one of the kids really "needs," and her mother-in-law gets such a thrill at being the one to make the great find. It makes her feel important—and needed.

"My in-laws are awesome at being grandparents!" my friend says. "This is what changed my relationship with my mom-in-law. She became a completely different person when we brought kids into the picture."

If having a child has improved your relationship with your mom-in-law, count your blessings!

Delicate Issues

Some women brought up some issues that I just don't have the know-how to deal with. Some of these situations are just going to require lots and lots of extra prayer and patience. Some will take some honest communication with the offending party and even more patience. Some might involve getting some answers from a counselor, pastor, or some other trusted expert.

"My in-laws and parents are both great grandparents!" says one friend. "With one small problem. Our two-year-old often repeats what my father-in-law says, and some of the things he says aren't the best."

"My husband and I are uncomfortable with his stepdad," says one woman, pregnant with her first baby. "His character is very questionable, and we won't be leaving our child alone with them at any time. My mother-in-law will likely have a problem with that."

Another friend lives in Australia while her family makes their home in England. "It makes me sad to think that my family won't be nearby to see their grandchildren grow up," she says. "It just makes me really teary thinking that they won't be here."

"Both are great grandparents," says one friend. "Our big problem is we will not allow my mother-in-law to babysit due to a serious health condition she has. She is unable to walk safely, she is partially blind, and she can't hold our baby unless she's sitting down. She doesn't see any problems with her watching him, but we have had big issues with her and the baby even when we were there. My husband was the one who decided she was not physically able to watch our son, and I agreed. This will probably cause more problems in the future."

"My two-year-old has quickly recognized a power struggle between my mom and me" says another friend. "She manipulates this to the best of her ability."

Another woman, a newlywed, is already anticipating problems with her in-laws when she and her husband decide to start having children. "His parents insist that if we have a girl, we have to use a certain family name," she says. "I literally want to vomit when I think about it. No one should be allowed to force me to name my child anything other than what my husband and I decide."

"We don't have kids yet," said one woman, "but my in-laws are a problem with the grandkids they already have. They use birthday and Christmas gifts as a way to manipulate them. I don't see my kids being close to them—ever."

If you have any great advice for these gals, write me, and I'll pass it on!

Mothers and Daughters

I love little boys to death, but whenever the subject of in-laws comes up, I can't help but be thankful I have all girls. I will never have a daughter-in-law, and I can't say I'm the least bit upset by this fact. Even better said, I will never be a mother-in-law to a young woman, and this is a very good thing.

I think grand-parenting is trickier with your sons' children than with your daughters' children. I have had so many women tell me their mothers-in-law show favoritism toward their daughters' kids.

And on the other hand, I've heard grandmas tell me about their daughters-in-law who seem to purposely make it difficult for their kids to have a relationship with them.

Let me use some fictional names and share a real example. Emily is married to Dan. Dan has a sister, Denise. This makes Emily and Denise sisters-in-law. Both women have a two-year-old daughter.

When I asked Emily to share a bit about her in-law dynamic when it comes to kids, she had a lot to say. "I could go on and on and on about my sister-in-law, whom I love but would also like to see go away sometimes. It's a love-hate relationship. I love when it's just the two of us. We get along fine. But when we're with family, especially her parents, I feel like a crappy mom, and she often says things that cut me down."

There's more. "My sister-in-law and her daughter get a lot of attention from my in-laws—way more than my daughter gets—which kind of hurts sometimes. I know it's just because she asks for so much help and I don't like to ask, but still it hurts."

Another mom shared, "Recently, our kids received *much* fewer presents at Christmas than my husband's sister's children. And while it's not about the presents, it hurts a lot when you are nine. My son threw up after this incident, and it is very difficult to forgive."

"My in-laws don't seem to care much about our son," one woman told me, "either because he is a boy and they like girls better or because he is my husband's son and not their daughter's son. I am not sure which it is."

This one's especially tough, because—I'm going to sound like a broken record—every story has two sides.

Let's face it. As a general rule, moms are closer to their daughters than they are to their sons. You know how the saying goes—a son is a son until he takes a wife, a daughter is a daughter for the rest of her life.

In many (not all) cases, if your husband has a sister, your mom-in-law will naturally be closer to her daughter than to her son (your hubby). And really, girls, we don't want his mama to be all chummy with him anyway, do we?

We can't have it all.

Time-Sharing

If you struggled to divide your time equally between your family and his *before* children, oh boy! In for a treat, you are! And when step-families are involved on one or both sides, life gets even more stressful.

"My mom is extremely possessive of her time with the grandchildren," one woman told me, "and this has caused a lot of grief. I get very emotionally drained and stressed because I simply cannot make everyone happy."

She admits that she is biased toward her mom, a single mother whose grandkids are her greatest joy. "I don't want to deprive her of that, and I enjoy spending time with her more than anyone else, so it's a little selfish as well. I am taking any and all advice!"

One friend talked about the family adjustments she and her husband were making after moving a state away from both sets of parents. "We really miss some of the family we left behind and can't wait to see them again. Then others have a way of trying to make us feel miserable from 500 miles away. Setting good boundaries is a challenge. We're doing our best to be loving and compassionate without being doormats."

Another friend who is not yet a mom told me, "I know women across America will hate me for it, but my parents and in-laws are so fantastic that I'm pressed to come up with any foreseeable problems."

But then she foresaw one that just might come up. "The only issue we could have is trying to balance our time with both of our parents. My parents are (understandably) jealous of the time they get to spend with us (especially now since we're far away), and they might get upset if they don't feel we're doling out baby-time fairly."

Communication with your husband is priority numero uno. And compromise is a close second. If you can clearly (and calmly) communicate and consistently compromise (oh, the alliteration!), you're one step ahead of the game.

Happy Holidays

I have four friends named Jessica. Two of them share the same opinion about the holidays—those special times of the year we all love and cherish.

"Holidays are the worst part about being married," said one Jessica. "Maybe the only bad part."

"We argue every holiday," said the other. "Holidays are horrible. I hate them."

My Jessicas are not alone.

"Holidays are awful," said another friend. "Both of our families live in the same town, and we live a state away. We can't very well travel four hours to see one family and not the other. But traveling back and forth a million times each day to divide our time evenly is exhausting."

"We live 45 minutes from mine and two hours from his," explained one friend. "His family acts uninterested and does not pursue us at all…except on big holidays, where they like to throw huge fits about the equality of time spent."

"We live about 45 minutes from my family and his," said one friend, "but in opposite directions. We don't measure the time, really, although his mother is always trying to find out where we are or assumes we are spending more time with my side. We now alternate for every holiday to keep everyone happy, although my mother-in-law will always let us know how they are inconvenienced or alone—even when it's not their turn."

One friend had an interesting solution. "We have Christmas in December with my family and Christmas in May with his. It is kind of strange, but we will have to get used to it."

The general consensus is that as your family grows and your kids get older, you slowly wean yourself away from celebrating Christmas at seven different places (yes, we do this every year) and start centering your holiday traditions around your own little family unit. How and when this happens can be tricky and sticky.

Best of luck with it! May your parents and in-laws (and aunts and uncles) be understanding!

A Quick Recap

Okay, so what did you learn in this chapter? Let me break it down for you into ten "easy" steps.

1. Put yourself in your in-laws' shoes.
2. Err on the side of loving.
3. Don't use or abuse your child's grandparents.
4. *You* take the first step toward a good relationship.
5. Communicate honestly and often with hubby.
6. Communicate honestly and often with parents and in-laws.
7. Compromise is key.
8. Send pride packing.
9. Encourage equal love for grandparents.
10. Pray for wisdom and patience and love.

Life isn't fair, and we weren't all blessed with fabulous extended families. But we always have room for improvement, and with God all things are possible. It's up to you to commit to do your part, and don't expect each side to go halfway. You go 100 percent and leave the results up to God.

Finding
Peace

7

Who Am I?

Raise your hand if you're a stay-at-home mom with a college degree in something other than motherhood. Wow—that's a lot of you.

Now, raise your hand if you think motherhood is a valuable and worthy endeavor. Good—all hands up.

And finally, raise your hand if you have a true sense of peace about what you're doing with your life right now. You feel fulfilled at all times, confident that you're living out life's highest calling. You never struggle with shame or embarrassment when people ask what you do for a living. You don't long for recognition or validation outside of motherhood. Your heart never aches for something...*bigger* than being a mom.

Raise those hands, and raise 'em high.

Hmm...just like I thought. Why is everybody sitting on her hands?

We know what we do is important, right? We don't need a paycheck to validate our worth, right? We know how significant our "career choice" is, right?

Sure, we *know*. But it's one thing to know something in our heads. It's another to feel it in our hearts.

On most good days, our hearts overflow with thankfulness for our children and for the privilege of being their mommy. On bad days, we wonder how in the world intelligent women like us got roped into the hardest, most thankless job in the history of the universe.

The Biggest Loser?

A few months after my first book was published, I got an e-mail from Jenny, an old high school classmate. We'd been friends in school but hadn't kept in touch in the 12 years since we'd graduated.

She told me she loved the book and got so much out of it. She said she had been reading my blog, and it felt like old times.

"I must admit I was feeling like a little bit of a loser," she wrote, "to read a book by someone I went to school with, when I was just at home nursing my third baby. But I quickly got over that. Your book was truly a blessing to me, and I pray it will bless many others. I'm glad I know you!"

Her words touched my heart, and I immediately replied with what I hope was an affirming and encouraging e-mail.

"I'm sitting here at home nursing my third baby too!" was part of what I wrote.

I tried my best to make her see what a wonderful, noble, beautiful, valuable thing she was doing. I felt so bad that my modest accomplishment would make one of my friends feel like a loser.

I remember briefly feeling the same way when I learned that one of my fellow small-college graduates was making it big as a sports broadcaster on TV. *Man,* I thought, *my life seems so small compared to hers.*

Oh, that comparison game is a deadly one. Nobody *ever* wins that one. And no one escapes unharmed.

If we are following Christ, and we know we're doing exactly what He has called us to do at this point in our lives, we are doing something brilliant! Successful! Fabulous! Remarkable! Boob sharer, book writer, or broadcaster—it makes no difference. To follow Christ and live smack in the center of God's will—it doesn't get any better than that!

But even though we know we should be finding our identities in

Christ and that it's all about Him, not about us, this concept some-times gets lost (or at least fuzzy) on the long trip from our heads to our hearts.

Reminding ourselves of these truths is a day-to-day job.

Just a Mom?

My friend Krista was at Bible study one night, having a wonderful time with some friends. A lady from church who had never seen her in this particular setting approached her as the evening ended. "Krista," she said, in a shocked voice, "you have quite a personality."

A little puzzled, Krista smiled and said "thanks."

"I have never spent any time with you where you aren't dealing with one of your children," the woman told her. "You have a sense of humor. You have a personality."

Krista laughed. I might have hauled off and hit the woman.

"I have often felt like I don't know who I am," says my friend Rachael. "I'm a mom, and that's it. I don't have a career. I don't have any huge accomplishments for a résumé. I don't even have any hobbies. So I do often feel like I don't have much of an identity. I'm my kids' mom, or my husband's wife, or whatever the title, but I'm not Rachael all that often. It's weird, but I do really appreciate people using my name when they speak to me because sometimes, I just forget."

"The first time someone called me Lily's mom felt really odd," Beki says. "My name was completely gone. I will never forget that feeling of, *Oh no!* I'm totally okay with it now. I know who I am, and I'm proud to be Lily's mom."

"I feel invisible sometimes when people talk to my baby and not me!" one friend told me.

Feeling invisible is one of the worst feelings ever. We all have a deep desire to know and be known. We want to be interesting, someone people like to converse with and want to get to know. We'd love for others to find us fascinating. We want our kids to think we're fun.

My friend Kristen told me recently that she's been feeling intro-spective, searching for significance. "My head knows that I find that in Christ," she said, "and that being a mom is the best thing I could be doing right now, but my heart longs for more. I want to do something great, something that impacts people and makes a positive difference in their lives.

"I want to feel like people in my life are proud of me and the job I have done. Some of this is pride, some may be a calling to something else, and somehow I have to figure out the difference and what to do about it. And yet I have about three minutes a day to think on these things."

Oh, what a paradox. There really are no easy solutions. And with each new generation, the challenges of being a mom seem to increase tenfold.

We have more questions than we have answers. Who am I? Why am I here? What is my life's purpose? Do I matter? Why don't I feel like I'm worth anything of value?

The Case of the Missing Identity

"I don't know how it happened," says my cousin Kyla, shaking her head, "but I really am a different person now." Becoming a mom to adorable little Rade last spring changed Kyla's life forever. You know the feeling.

Some of those changes you welcome with open arms. Your heart is bigger. Your eyes are opened wider than ever before. (Well, figuratively speaking, anyway. In literal terms, you can't keep your eyes open for the life of you.) You can't imagine life without your precious child.

But other changes are a little harder to accept—your new body, the constant sacrifice, the postponed career, the exhaustion, the lack of time or opportunity to do the things you once loved, the new way people perceive you (whether it's real or imagined).

Listen in on some more moms who struggled to figure out who they were and where they fit once their babies came into the world. I love that you can just feel their hearts seeping out of their gut-honest words.

"I was very young, and none of my friends had kids," says Kristen.

"So I felt as if I was excluded from the club. I didn't fit in with the mom club because I wasn't old enough (and didn't have a van), but I didn't fit in with the college kids either because our lives were suddenly so different."

"I felt so, so odd," says Jessica C. "I just remember feeling like I was in some weird identity cloud. I knew how to use my gifts in a business environment, but figuring them out at home was hard."

"Motherhood has changed my identity," says Megan. "Before having my son, I was a wife, the youth pastor's wife, a teacher. Now, I'm a wife, a mom, the youth pastor's wife. That is a really significant change when you work with teens. They don't often understand why I can't do all the things I used to do."

"I often feel like I don't know who I am," one woman said. "But that's what being a mother is—sacrifice. If you want to do it and do it right, it's a constant sacrifice."

"I feel like almost everything I do is for someone else," another mom told me. "I don't even remember what life was like before my son was born. To be honest, I don't even really remember what I used to do with my time."

"Yes, I often feel like I don't know who I am," said one woman. "Especially when I haven't had any time for myself for what seems like months, when it's the same thing day in and day out and there seems to be no hope for anything different."

"Sometimes I feel like just a mother," another woman told me, "and not the pretty, attractive woman my husband first met. Sometimes I feel like I'm no longer cool and fun loving. Not all the time, mostly just when I'm overwhelmed."

"In my own way, I think I felt as if motherhood would fill a void in my life," says one woman. "That definitely didn't happen. It made it worse. I loved being a mother, but it was so much harder than I ever anticipated."

"In times of sheer frustration, things take on a life of their own," another mom said. "Certainly at times I do wonder if I'm still in there!"

"I feel important because I know I am a huge factor in shaping who Leah is becoming," says Missy. "But I do feel lost a lot and wonder when I will get myself back. I feel like I have to be eternally selfless to care for Leah and do everything I'm supposed to for the family and around the house. I know this isn't the case because I can be pretty selfish, but I still feel that way at times. Sometimes I feel as if I don't exist in the sense that my needs and wants are the last to be met or the first to be ignored."

"My biggest challenge has been defining myself," Samantha says. "A dear friend gave me some great advice that has helped me through this. It is not what I am *doing* but who I am *being* that matters."

It's who you are *being* that matters.

Your Other Parts

I think part of the problem is that we women are multifaceted creatures. We play so many roles in life, or at least we want to. When our kids are small, they take up so much time and energy that those other parts get lost. We feel most complete when all those parts are there.

Sara, mom to two little girls, has a great outlook on this. "I am a child of God who happens to wear many hats," she says. "They don't always match the outfit I want to wear! But somehow they always fit. I am a mother, yes, but I am so much more than that. I am a wife, a friend, a lover, an employee, a sister, a daughter, a woman. My daughters get to see me being all these things while still being their mom. I love being all of these things!"

The hard part is trying to wear all those hats without dropping any of them. As Sara said, they don't always match what she wants to wear! I personally would like to wear the "sit down in peace and read a novel while sipping coffee" hat a lot more often than I get to!

Listen in on some moms who are working through this very thing. Some of them have found some ways to revive their other parts. Some of them haven't yet. The process is ongoing, and knowing when to be self-sacrificing and when it's okay to take time for you is rarely easy.

"I never feel like I don't know who I am," one woman said. "but I do wonder if I am living up to my potential because I haven't had time to do other things I could be doing."

"I used to love to do crafts," says one woman, "and I don't get to do much of that anymore. I can't knit or crochet at night because my daughter wants to sit on my lap. Sometimes that gets frustrating, but I try to keep it in perspective and remember that she won't always want to sit with me."

"I do find at times that I need to stop and take time for myself," says Jill. "I throw myself into the lives of my little ones, and it can be easy to forget what I enjoy or what I am good at."

"Many of the dreams I had for music and a singing ministry have been put on the back burner," one woman said. "I grew up thinking I'd be out there singing all the time, and now it's once a month at church. It's been hard at times, and I've felt like I was wasting a God-given talent. I know He'll use me when it's my time."

"Motherhood has caused me to focus on myself less," says Julie. "I rarely put myself first. On some days I don't know who I am or what I want, and that concerns me. It's hard to know what God's purpose is for my life, other than being a mom."

"Motherhood has given me more of a sense of purpose in life," Shelly says. "I know that everything I do is making some sort of impression on my son. Of course, on some days I forget a bit about that purpose and feel like the same tasks over and over have no meaning."

"Yes, I often wonder who I am," says Anne Marie. "Sometimes I catch glimpses of things I used to love to do and try to do them more. I played on a coed soccer team and a softball team a few times recently. It was hard to squeeze in, but I felt like my old adventurous, carefree, athletic self. I try to reflect on days before mom-hood by journaling, scrapbooking, and doing a journal jar. It is important to retain some things you really enjoy doing."

I'm Alone. Now What?

One of the craziest paradoxes in all of motherhood is our desperate need to get a break from our children and the desperate longing we feel for them when we're finally away.

Take Jennifer and her husband for example. Living as missionaries in Japan, they hadn't gotten away on a date alone since before ten-month-old Ana was born. When family came for a visit, Jenn and her hubby left Ana in good hands and escaped for dinner and a movie.

"As excited as I was about this before it took place," Jenn says, "I still cried all the way to the restaurant and up until the server brought out our food, all the while thinking about Ana and how much I missed her. I didn't even know to prepare for this irony before she was born. Anyway, I did manage to pull myself together, and it was a wonderful evening."

I remember pumping a boatload of milk for my first overnighter away from my youngest when she was seven months old. With each whir of the pump, I thought, *Oh, I don't think I'm ready for this yet.* I was a little nervous, a little sad, but thrilled to have 36(!) child-free hours with my hubby.

Anytime I'm away from my girls overnight, I get this twinge—almost painful—of *can I really leave them and go away?* They're seven, five, and two now, and it's still not easy.

Sarah says, "Sometimes I am so tired that I just want time to myself, but when I do get away, I don't know what to do with myself apart from my baby."

"I feel like I don't know what I like to do anymore," Krista says. "When my husband gives me an afternoon to go out and do whatever I want, I sometimes struggle to come up with anything to do. I usually end up window-shopping, getting a coffee, and watching people."

"I am probably more comfortable with 'Tracy the mom' than 'Tracy the woman,'" says one gal. "I'm not sure why, but I know I often like to take at least one of the kids to the store with me to maintain my 'mom' identity."

I do the same thing. When I'm shopping for groceries alone, I find myself smiling at moms and their little ones. And I get this crazy urge to say, "I'm a mom too! Just like you!"

And when I take just one and not two or all three, I think, *These people are going to think I only have one child and that my life is easy!* Heaven forbid.

Should I Stay or Should I Go?

I haven't really talked much up to this point about the decision to be a stay-at-home mom or a working mom. Now is a good time to broach the subject. A topic hotter than breast-feeding, co-sleeping, and babywise combined (more on those in chapter 9).

So what do you do if you really don't want to stay home? Am I going to condemn you for that?

Let's just say that this book is not about judgment and making moms feel guilty for the choices they have made. I'd be crushed to find out that a mom closed this book feeling angry, hurt, or attacked.

The question of the hour: Should I be a working mom or a stay-at-home (SAH) mom? Of course, there are all sorts of variations—working part-time, working from home, dad staying at home with baby, grandma watching the kids, day care...

Every situation is different. We know this. And you know what I've chosen for my family, so that's no secret. I left a teaching career to stay at home with my girls, started getting paid to write from home, and plan to continue indefinitely.

Even when all my girls are in school all day, I have no desire to go back to teaching. I still have all kinds of teaching opportunities—just in different settings these days.

My goal for this chapter is not to persuade you to quit your job and stay at home with your kids. My goal is not to subtly share what you're missing out on if you choose to have a career.

Yes, I think that staying home with your kids is ideal. But so is feeding them healthy foods, and my kids eat quite a bit of junk.

Many women have no choice but to work. Your husband's job doesn't have benefits. Or you can't pay your mortgage on his salary alone. Or you're a single mom.

You have to do what you feel God is calling you to do. You answer to Him and your family alone. What I (or anyone else) think about your decision is really irrelevant. Consult with God and your family, and make your choice.

There is *no* need for working moms and SAH moms to say things to each other that are belittling or condescending. For example, if you work outside the home, saying something like this to an SAH mom is unacceptable: "My mind is just too active to stay at home and play all day." (Yes, someone actually said this to a gal I know.)

That's clearly lame and a low blow at that, insinuating that dumb women stay home and play with their kids while the smart ones go out and work at real jobs. Whose mind *isn't* too active to stay at home and play all day? You can find plenty of ways to make sure your mind gets a workout. You just have to be creative.

And for an SAH mom to say something like this to a working mom would be just as unacceptable: "I'd love to get out of the house all day too, but I've chosen to actually *be* there for my children." (Don't even think about it.)

Cutting remarks like that serve no helpful purpose. None. If you make a choice you believe is best for your family, and that choice is based on lots of prayer and honest communication with your husband, you never need to apologize to anyone. And you certainly don't need to belittle anyone else for her personal choice. No exceptions.

Again, stay tuned for chapter 9—all about loving each other as moms despite our different choices.

All to His Glory

One young mom expressed her mixed emotions about being home with her daughter. "I ended up being a stay-at-home mom," she says, "but I don't think it's a permanent choice. I love being with my little girl, but I hate being cooped up in the house and repeatedly doing the same unpaid chores."

She expressed her desire to finish college online and then find a career that would enable her to work from home or in a kid-friendly environment.

This young mom had a job before her baby was born, and the transition was admittedly hard for her. "I'm used to being productive and self-motivated and a leader," she says. "I feel as though all of that has been turned on its head. Finding motivation to do the dishes *again* after I just did them escapes me. I used to be all about keeping my living spaces spic and span, but I seem to fail to care anymore. Staying at home has been a very depressing, lonely experience and one that I hope will soon come to an end. I love being a mom. I just hate being home all the time."

We've all felt like this. It takes some kind of woman to stay motivated to do dishes on a daily basis.

But after three summers as a camper and two as a counselor, our church camp motto rings in my head at times like these. "So whether you eat or drink or whatever you do, do it all for the glory of God" (1 Corinthians 10:31).

Dishes and diaper changing and laundry and toilet scrubbing definitely fit under the heading of "whatever you do." Looking at our menial tasks as ways to bring God glory and even worship Him makes them so much more bearable.

I love these words Paul has for the Romans. "So here's what I want you to do," he says, "God helping you: Take your everyday, ordinary life—your sleeping, eating, going-to-work, and walking-around life— and place it before God as an offering. Embracing what God does for you is the best thing you can do for him" (12:1 MSG).

My sister-in-law Jess is inspiring to me as a mom. She has been so honest about the changes God has worked in her heart lately.

Before she met my brother, she was on track to graduate from college, get her master's, and pursue some wildly successful career. Then she met Josh, fell in love, and married young. Still hope for that fab career though, right?

Then she got pregnant a year later. The life of a youth pastor's wife with a baby put her career on hold. She took some classes and made some plans to continue her education, and then baby number two came along. Then baby number three.

One of Jess's prayers was that God would bring something fulfilling into her life. I love the way He granted her wish.

"I just took some delicious banana muffins out of the oven," she told me recently, "and I still have a loaf of banana bread cooking. I feel like such a homemaker today. My house is (pretty much on its way to being) clean, and I'm learning to knit, baking, playing games, and reading books with my kiddies. What a life! I love my life!"

Then she explained how she came to a place of such contentment. "God had to do a lot of work on me," she said, "to make me truly content being a mom who stays home and just takes care of house and kids. But I'm so glad He answered my prayers *His* way when I prayed, *Give me something that is truly fulfilling!* I was hoping He'd give me a job I could do from home or something like that. But instead He gave me a great sense of His purpose in raising up another generation of people who love Christ! What could be better than that? I guess it's just God allowing me to be content doing exactly what He wants me to do!"

Jess is placing her life before God as an offering.

Go with God

It comes down to this: We each have a decision to make. Pursue the career or stay home with our kids. Or try to tackle both at once. The way this plays out in each woman's life is going to be different.

We all need to take some important steps before making a final decision. First and foremost, cover it in prayer. We shouldn't make any decision—let alone a monumental one like this one—without asking God for His opinion. Search His Word, talk to Him, wait for peace.

And true peace will never come if you're going against God's Word or what you feel He's specifically telling you to do.

And I firmly believe you and your husband need to be on the same page. Does he want you working or home with the kids? If you can't agree, pray that God will change one of your hearts. Compile a list of reasons why you feel your choice is best for your family. Share it with him when you feel the time is right—and after you've spent time in prayer.

And last, ask yourself what's best for your entire family. Not just one person, but everyone. This is the decision you need to go with. And look ahead to the future too. How do my choices now affect our future as a family?

Words of Inspiration

Have you ever seen the movie *Chariots of Fire?* Me neither, but I've heard it's great. And I love the quote from the main character, a runner, who says, "When I run, I feel His pleasure!"

These next few quotes remind me of that. When these moms do the mom thing, they feel God's pleasure. And they inspire me to love the life God has called me to live—the life of a mama.

"I love being a mom! Love it!" says my friend Faith. "I am what I always dreamed I'd be! I have so much more confidence, and I feel like I have a purpose now. I have a clear job and a goal—to raise God-honoring kids—and it's wonderful. Plus, considering my introverted ways, now I always have a conversation piece!"

"I don't think that motherhood has made me question my identity," says Claudia. "If anything, it has helped me recognize my strengths and weaknesses and better understand who I am."

"Motherhood really changed me for the better," one mom says. "I've never felt so fulfilled or so worthwhile as when I had this little person to nurture, love, and help develop."

"Motherhood hasn't really changed my identity as a person," one woman said. "I am still the same person—I just have more love in my heart."

"I think motherhood has enhanced my identity," another woman told me. "I can see daily that I'm making a difference in my kids' lives, and it motivates me and holds me accountable."

"I think my daughter has given me an even stronger identity than I had before," says one mom. "I am so much more important because

I am her mother. I have such a great responsibility to teach her things and guide her."

"I know this is something a lot of women struggle with," says Cherith, "but I don't think I have a problem with my identity being 'mom.' Maybe it's because I never really had a career or anything that I gave up, or maybe it's because I always knew that when I had kids I would stay home with them, so my expectations weren't for anything grander."

"I feel like this is what I've been waiting my whole life to do," says Suzanne, "even though I sometimes feel inadequate and unprepared."

"I had no idea how selfish I was until I had a baby!" Jennifer F. says. "My daughter challenges me to be better in all areas of my life so that I can be the best example of a godly woman to her. I did feel for a while that I didn't know who I was, but I've since realized that any changes in my life have been for the better. She is God's little convicting gift to me!"

"I am more dimensional because I am a mom," says Terri. "I became a better, more empathetic teacher as my own boys grew. I believe being a mom, and now a 'Mamaw,' simply adds more spice to my stew."

"My boys bring me so much joy and such a sense of fulfillment," Kristen says. "The everyday tasks of feeding, clothing, doing laundry, and cleaning toilets can get so mundane and seem so pointless at times, but when you look at the big picture, those things bring the most security to our families. We take care of their daily needs, and while the work may be taken for granted and constantly need doing, ultimately it is providing stability in the home that is the foundation for almost everything else. There may be no praise and little gratitude, but it provides an opportunity to love on a new level—selflessly."

God's Words of Inspiration

I love closing a chapter with some fresh words from the Lord for you. I don't have enough space to write all I want to say. I want so badly to express to you what an amazing calling motherhood is, what a valuable thing it is that you're doing, that nothing on earth compares to nurturing a baby into a full-grown, Christ-following adult.

Just chew on some of these incredible verses (all from The Message) that speak to our need to matter. We do matter. We matter to all kinds of people for all kinds of reasons. But if nothing else, we matter like crazy to the God who created us and will love us for all eternity!

"Throw yourselves into the work of the Master," Paul encourages his readers in 1 Corinthians 15:58, "confident that nothing you do for him is a waste of time or effort."

Nothing we do for Him is a waste! Nothing. And especially not the crucial task of being a mom.

Remember all our talk about losing ourselves, wanting to find out who we are, feeling lost? Jesus has an answer to that in Matthew 10:39. "If your first concern is to look after yourself, you'll never find yourself," He says. "But if you forget about yourself and look to me, you'll find both yourself and me."

Paul believed these words and constantly shared them with others. "It's in Christ that we find out who we are and what we are living for" (Ephesians 1:11).

It may seem like a trite statement to you—find your identity in Christ—but friend, when you do, it will change your life.

Who *are* you? If you have accepted Christ as your Savior, you are a child of God, loved and cherished and forgiven and redeemed.

You matter. Oh, how you matter.

8

Nondenominational Motherhood

Motherhood has more denominations than the Protestant church. And each of us usually thinks her mommy doctrinal statement is superior to the rest.

We can all too easily get caught up in competing with each other, comparing ourselves to one another, and judging anyone who does things differently than we do.

I'm going to make a bold statement: Believe it or not, I think we moms can all get along, regardless of our parenting philosophies.

I think we can choose to nurse our babies or bottle-feed, rock our babies or let them cry it out, wear our babies or wear bikinis, and so on (and on and on) and still love each other as fellow travelers on the same journey.

Yes, I have my own ideas about how parenting should work (at least in theory, even if I can't seem to implement all of them in real life). But I'm not here to criticize your personal mothering choices—not for a minute.

For the purposes of this book, I'm claiming nondenominational motherhood. I'm just going to sit up here on the fence, straddle it happily, and do what I can to appeal to moms on both sides.

I'm not out to make anybody mad. I'm here to uplift, encourage, and get you chuckling a time or two.

Even still, you may not like certain parts of this chapter. That's fine. If you agreed with everything I said, I'd be a little suspect. Much of what I say is personal opinion, just one woman's point of view. No two people see the world in general or motherhood in particular exactly the same.

We are Christ followers before we are mothers. We've got to remember that. And if our hearts are right before Him, if our ears are open to hear His voice and we're obeying, the mothering choices we make are secondary.

And in the words of my wise cousin Kyla, "Moms should be more supportive of each other. As women, we are all unique. As moms, we are equally unique. So unless someone's feeding the baby Mountain Dew and crack for breakfast, ease up."

Paul speaks to our God-created uniqueness in his letter to the Romans. "So since we find ourselves fashioned into all these excellently formed and marvelously functioning parts in Christ's body, let's just go ahead and be what we were made to be, without enviously or pridefully comparing ourselves with each other, or trying to be something we aren't" (12:5-6 MSG).

So, my marvelously functioning friend, let's dig right in to some of those mommy topics that tend to divide us. And while we're at it, let's discover how we can have true compassion for our fellow travelers along the way.

Not All Boobs Are Created Equal

I'm going to tackle one of the biggest issues first and move on. The great debate: breast or bottle? I'll spare you the fact sheet. We all know by now that breast milk is the original recipe. All other milk is second best.

Yet some moms see breast-feeding as the be-all and end-all of motherhood. It's boobs or nothing.

They wouldn't dream of giving their babies a drop of formula. They even hate the thought of giving them breast milk in a bottle. They won't introduce solid foods until the last possible moment. They relish the fact that their baby's chubby cheeks are chubby for one reason only—mama's milk. And they make sure everyone knows it. They nurse for well over a year, sometimes two or three.

This is all perfectly fine. But many moms take it one step too far. They look down their noses at anyone who doesn't breast-feed. The unspoken message: If you don't nurse your baby (and do it long enough), you obviously don't have your baby's best interests at heart. You're not a good mom. Period.

So before we go any further, how about we all check our judgmental attitudes right here at the door?

Lest I sound like I'm anti-boob-feeding, let me assure you that I nursed all three of my girls and loved every minute of it. It was by far my favorite part of having babies. I'd have another one right this very second just so I could nurse again. I loved the bonding, the closeness, the sensation, the miracle of producing exactly what my baby needed when no one else could.

But I used to (wrongly) assume that every woman who wanted to breast feed would be able to do it. I now know that this is absolutely not the case. I know many women who would have given an arm and a leg for breasts that could feed their babies, and after much pain and crying and anguish, they gave up their dream.

And as if the disappointment and feelings of failure weren't enough, they had to deal with insensitive people who tsk-tsked them for their "selfish decision."

One good friend came home from the hospital with her baby girl and felt completely overwhelmed by the responsibility before her. "This little infant wanted nothing to do with my boobs!" she says. "She could have starved to death! She wouldn't nurse. She would rear her head back and wail. Move her head side to side and scream. No matter how many nurses or lactation consultants or friends tried to help me, she wouldn't latch on. I felt like a failure, like we couldn't bond. I took about six weeks to finally realize it was okay to just pump milk so neither of us would end up in tears over it."

I recently talked to another friend whose breast-feeding difficulties were very fresh in her mind. With her first child, she developed a horrible infection that led to two surgeries, and with her second, she had other difficulties she couldn't overcome.

"I'm the biggest supporter of breast-feeding," she said. (It's true.) "I think it's so important for babies to get their mommy's milk. It doesn't work for everyone though. I wish people would get that."

She was on a roll, so I let her go. "I don't care if 'Jesus was breast-fed,'" she said. "I really don't. Formula is not poison. There is more to motherhood than breast milk!"

I think we need to start looking at breast-feeding as a *gift*. And not every woman has it. Is breast milk best? Maybe so, but I think we're all mature enough to realize that in life, we don't always get what's best, and that's okay.

Yes, breast-feeding is glorified in the Bible. But so is childbearing, and some women are infertile. Adoption isn't second-best motherhood. Neither is feeding your baby formula.

I know women who chose not to breast-feed for reasons as different as night and day. These women love their babies like crazy. These babies love their mamas. All is well. Everyone is healthy. When all was said and done, no one lost any brain cells. (If anyone loses brain cells, it's nursing mothers!)

In my friend's case, breast-feeding was causing her (and her baby and husband) all kinds of stress and anxiety, so she stopped.

"I suppose my feelings are so strong about it because I always thought I would nurse for at least six months to a year. And it didn't work for me with either of my babies. I went to the ends of the earth the first time to try to nurse my daughter, but she wouldn't latch on. I tried again with my son—same problem. So I pumped for two months. But it wasn't working in the whole balance of our family, so I gave it up. Bottle-feeling might not be the best choice, but as part of the whole picture of our lives, it's been for the best. I guess I just get sick of the moms who think moms who don't nurse don't love their kids."

I told her I loved her and that I'd be praying that the people with insensitive remarks on the tips of their tongues would stay far away from her—like the woman who had the audacity to tell my friend Jennifer F. that her nine-month-old was going to be fat one day because (and she said this directly to the baby girl) "Mommy didn't want to breast-feed you."

It's a good thing Jenn lives in Japan, or I would have been all over that woman.

Back to my friend who had trouble nursing. "I appreciate the fact that you get it," she told me. "Motherhood is the combination of a bunch of different things, and striking the right balance among all of them is what makes it work. I'm firm and confident in the decision, but it still helps tremendously to have support."

The Moral of the Story

Don't judge another mom *at all* unless you've walked a mile (or 50) in her shoes. And this especially holds true for breast-feeding.

And to take it even further, please be sensitive when you talk glowingly about breast-feeding. You know what I mean—how fabulous and easy it is and how your baby is just flourishing on mama's milk.

It's really no different from bragging about your soccer prowess or your perfect grade point average or how good you are in bed. Actually, it's even worse because of the sensitive nature of the topic. You never know who you're talking to—your words could crush someone who had her ever-lovin' heart set on breast-feeding and feels like the world's biggest failure because it didn't work out.

I'd love to have a dollar for every bumper sticker I've seen singing the praises of cloth diapers and home births and breast-fed kindergarteners. All noble endeavors, but they need to be tempered with love and acceptance.

I'd like to start my own line of bumper stickers. "Love comes from the heart, not the boobs," for example.

A few months ago, my friend Jennifer addressed the breast-feeding issue on her blog, and I asked her for permission to share her story. Her attitude is fabulous—feel free to take notes.

The other day I woke up with a 103-degree fever and a horrible pain in my right armpit. (Bonus points to you if you can name that ailment!) I thought it would get better, so I kept on nursing, but after a couple of feverish days, I realized that I was wrong. I'm on antibiotics now and quite done with the whole breast-feeding fiasco, part two, thankyouverymuch. I told Wes that if there's another little one in our future, he is to absolutely forbid me from even considering nursing as an option. Kudos to you ladies who are able to do it without losing your mind. I wish I knew your secret!

Last year, I felt like such a failure when I switched Ana to formula after only a week of nursing. So much so that I was depressed for a good long while and seriously doubted if I was even capable of taking care of and loving a baby.

This time? I was practically dancing a little freedom jig when I put that first bottle of formula in Emma's mouth. I just feel liberated. I know that I love this baby and that I'm capable of taking care of her. Or I'm assuming so, since the first one is still alive. Ana is clearly not mutated because she was fed formula. Unless, of course, she has some supernatural powers that I am unaware of at this point in time.

Don't you love how she genuinely applauds the women who breast-feed successfully but she doesn't let it get her down that she's not one of the lucky ones? Can we be big about this one? Can we forget about being lactivists and just laugh with each other? Can we love each other whether we nurse or not?

We can? Great!

To Rock or Not to Rock

Might as well jump right in to babywise (BW) versus attachment parenting (AP). Two popular parenting philosophies I'd describe as polar opposites of each other.

For those of you unfamiliar with these terms, let me give you the CliffsNotes version (off the top of my head).

The word *babywise* is coined from the book *On Becoming Baby Wise* by Gary Ezzo and Robert Bucknam. In a nutshell (don't shoot me if I'm not getting this all right), the popular version includes putting baby on a strict, disciplined eating and sleeping schedule (I'm assuming baby pees and poops on schedule too, but maybe not). Not rocking baby to sleep, but putting him into the crib awake. The baby learns to put himself to sleep. No co-sleeping, no carrying baby in a sling.

The idea behind this? Mom and Dad set the family's routine, not baby. Baby learns structure and discipline. She feels safe, has boundaries, and learns the independence necessary to survive in life (or at least preschool). And again, please no hate mail if I missed key points three and eight of the method. We're just talking generalities here.

Attachment parenting is just like it sounds. You are attached to your baby (often in a sling of some sort) unless you are showering, using the toilet, or cooking over a hot stove. Then again, I'm sure people find ways to wear the baby during these activities too.

You nurse your baby on demand. She cries—you nurse her. You nurse her to sleep, she sleeps in bed with you, you wear her in a sling during the day. AP babies wear cloth diapers, eat natural foods (after six months) and often breast-feed for several years before being weaned. Many AP babies are born at home or with midwives in birthing centers. Minimal intervention is optimal.

Why attachment parenting? For one thing, mothers use this method in many cultures around the world and have been using it for centuries. It's the natural way to mother—the way nature intended babies to be raised. The hope is that baby will feel safe, comfortable, secure, and loved.

Generally speaking, AP moms think babywise is cruel—doing what's best for the mother at the baby's expense. Many BW moms think the attachment moms are hippie freaks—creating children who think they're the center of the universe and will still sleep with their parents until they leave for college.

"You must not love your child," AP says.

"You're going to smother your child," says BW.

AP moms say BW moms are selfish. BW moms think AP moms are selfish too. After all, they just know the AP hubbies aren't getting any sex!

Marla says—can't we all just get along? Please?

Now, if your friend is Muslim and you want her to know Jesus, a push for conversion to Christianity may be in order. But even then, the best approach is love and prayer.

But if your baby is attached and your friend's is babywised, conversion isn't necessary. You both love God and have accepted Christ? Awesome. Agree to disagree on the parenting model and get on with your friendship!

I understand the desire to get together with other moms who speak your parenting language. If you're going the babywise route and want some support, advice, and encouragement, you can only get that from other babywise moms. And vice versa with the APers.

But make sure you're also reaching out and getting together with some moms who see things differently. And maybe you'll have to talk about something other than your kids. This is actually okay.

I can name a handful of gals I'd consider opposite extremes on the AP-BW continuum, and I love 'em all to death.

Unity in diversity suggests maturity. Did you catch all that? In other words, when you can love someone who thinks differently than you do, you're being mature.

"May our dependably steady and warmly personal God develop maturity in you," Paul tells the Romans (and us!), "so that you get along with each other as well as Jesus gets along with us all" (15:5 MSG).

Is There a Happy Medium?

This is where this business starts to get personally tricky. For me to promote a middle ground between the two "extreme" philosophies would be to go beyond just straddling my fence. It's the equivalent of telling you that the *only* place to be is riding the fence.

So I'll tell you what I did with my girls, but remember, I'm not saying it's best for everyone. You do what you gotta do. If someone asks for my opinion, I'll offer it, but I don't ever force it down anyone's throat.

I know you didn't technically ask for my opinion, but you *are* reading the book.

For me, I'm all about balance. I nursed my babies but stopped short of a year with all three. I rocked them to sleep (or nursed them to sleep) for months, but they made the transition pretty easily to falling asleep on their own (with a few awful screaming episodes). I never used a cloth diaper or a sling.

I fed entirely on demand—and I'm sure they ate plenty of times when they weren't even hungry. They were always off the charts for height and weight, but you would be too if your parents were tall and you ate 15 meals a day.

Let's see…what else? No home births. Two epidurals and one au naturel. No schedule to speak of. Flexible (okay, disorganized) routine. No babies in our bed except for the times I fell asleep nursing. Little girls with fevers in the middle of the night still come sleep in our bed so I don't have to kneel by theirs when I'm pooped. Anyone scared of loud thunderstorms is welcome too (until the storm passes, that is).

I think that about sums it up.

And as I said, I've got friends on both sides of the fence. And friends with a leg or a foot propped up on the fence. And friends who are fellow straddlers. It's all good.

I even have friends who tried one philosophy with their first child and then decided to try another one just for fun with their second.

So you may go strictly with one method or the other—or a myriad of ones I didn't even mention (because I don't know about them!)—or you can pick and choose and form your own little philosophy.

I do believe balance is best, but there are a million combinations to choose from. No mom's balance looks exactly like anyone else's.

Whatever you do, just be sure to show a little grace and compassion to the moms who go down a different path than you use. And who knows—they might actually have a thing or two to teach you about life on the trail.

Someday You'll Understand

Other moms aren't the only women we need to learn to get along with. Sadly, we girls often divide ourselves into two camps—not-yet moms (NYMs) and moms.

Things can be sailing smoothly between a NYM and a mom until the NYM dares to make an observation about the mom's parenting. Just an observation, mind you. Not even a piece of advice or criticism necessarily (although those happen too).

The mom turns to the NYM and says with a huff or an eye roll, "Someday you'll understand."

Let me share a mild (and true) example. Two sisters living on two different continents. Older sister is married with children. Younger sis is married without. Younger sis is reading up on whole fruit versus juice because her hubby is a juice lover. She finds that eating whole fruit is much healthier than drinking juice and that children should only have a small amount of juice daily. She shares her findings with older sis. Older sis is "offended by this personal attack." Younger sis honestly meant no harm.

When something like this happens, a mom (already insecure by nature, as most mothers are) feels threatened. She fires back those dreaded words "someday you'll understand," and a battle ensues.

Only recently did I realize what strong emotions that simple phrase invokes in a NYM when spoken (usually condescendingly) by a mom.

You might think I would naturally take the mom's side, and in some cases (each is different), I do. But I can definitely see both angles.

From the mom's perspective, let me try to explain the phrase as best I can. Here's the deal. No one (mom *or* NYM) likes to go through something really tough and then have others downplay the difficulty of this particular thing. And we really, really don't like it when someone insinuates that she would have handled things differently (that is, better).

Motherhood is tough, and we don't feel validated in our role unless everyone around us recognizes that fact, empathizes with us, and gives us the respect we believe we're due.

So when someone without children questions our parenting decisions or skills (or it even remotely seems like they possibly might be doing so), those defensive juices immediately come bubbling to the surface. We simply cannot bear to bite our tongues or let the comments slide.

So we do the worst thing possible. We announce (in a condescending tone, no less) the fact that we will bite our tongues or let it slide because "someday, you'll understand." We imply that it isn't even worth the effort to try to explain it at this juncture because how in tarnation could a NYM *possibly* understand?

When it comes to our children and the job we're doing as their mothers, we're no ducks. Let remarks roll off our feathery backs? Fuhgeddaboutit.

Why NYMs Resent This Phrase

Let me take a moment to defend the NYMs who are offended by moms who tell them they'll understand someday.

Moms, first of all, how many of you have used this phrase? I know, I know, sometimes you say it without thinking and without a hint of malice. But other times—admit it!—you say it to get under someone's skin. You're trying to get back at her for what you took as an affront to your parenting skills.

Here's how NYMs feel when you use this line. (We'll start with some women who are only mildly offended.)

> "I feel a tad frustrated that they think I am totally oblivious to what it is like to be a mother. But I probably really don't know much of the sacrifice and joy that it is! I pray that someday I do!"

> "I think moms have every right to say that, don't get me wrong. I don't like hearing it, but I have a feeling that maybe someday I *will* understand."

"It's sort of patronizing, but I guess it's true. For me, I really don't pretend to understand what motherhood is going to be like."

"To some degree I agree with this line of thinking—you can't fully understand until you experience it. But (most) women are just naturally maternal, and whether they have kids or not, mom instincts are there."

"I feel like they feel they are superior to me. I never act like I think I know anything, so for someone to say that to me is annoying. It can be said without being condescending, though, and that doesn't bother me."

"As long as they're not saying it condescendingly (as if I was an idiot for simply being in a different phase in my life than they are), I don't mind a single bit."

"Drives me nuts when it is used against me and held over me as though I will never understand such and such issue until I push a baby out. However, there is some truth to it; I just don't like when it is used the wrong way."

"I'm fully aware that I don't understand what it's like to be a parent. I'm a nanny, an aunt, a cousin, and stuff like that, but not a mother. There's a difference between knowing and understanding. I know that being a mother is hard, but I don't understand it. I know that mothers of babies are up all night and sleep deprived, but I don't understand it."

"I know they understand things now that I really can't comprehend, but it is still belittling. There must be a better way to offer advice."

And then there are some women who are deeply offended by the statement and are more than happy to share the reasons why.

"I find it extremely condescending to be spoken down to as such. It implies that because someone has given birth they are completely in the know and I could not possibly have any applicable thoughts or insights based on watching and learning over time. It automatically insinuates that I am incorrect or ignorant or naive in my opinion. And while that may be true, it's okay for me to have such an opinion. It's generally considered rude to imply such things to someone about non-parental topics; this should be no different."

"Don't even get me started…Obviously, there are things I won't fully understand until I'm there 24/7, but I can sympathize and relate even though I'm not a mom. I have been puked on, pooped on, peed on, spit on, bitten (although not there), kicked, hit, awake all night, and exhausted. That phrase makes me feel itty-bitty and less valid as a person and even more so as a woman and future mom."

"This statement makes me extremely angry and resentful. I am an oldest child who likes to figure things out for myself. I don't like when people give me advice—I see it as criticism. I think that the only thing a mother has over me is the fact that she is older or just happened to have a baby before me and may be a little more experienced with caring for her child. Perhaps I am just as capable of being as good a mother (if not a better) than this woman when the time comes for me to be a mom."

I know almost all of these women personally. These are not bitter women. They don't have chips on their shoulders. They all dream of becoming mothers someday and genuinely feel belittled when women who are already moms tell them they can't possibly understand what it's like.

My cousin Kelly, a NYM, has some brilliant insight I'd like to share. I hesitate to label her a NYM because she practically raised a relative of hers for the first few years of his life. Please, enjoy her words of wisdom.

That statement is dumb, and it can be irritating. It's like dismissing a person as invalid and smugly excluding her from your little mommy club (especially when the statement is accompanied by that little knowing and annoying smile). If you think it, fine. But it doesn't need to be said.

I think some mothers (especially new moms) are just really smug over the fact that they have birthed a child, and they want to lord it over those who haven't. They're enamored with motherhood as if they were the first ones ever to accomplish such a feat.

Also, there is the possibility that maybe the non-mother won't ever understand. I mean, I know tons of mothers who think that other moms are idiots for the way they do things. Not all kids and babies act the same, and there are many styles of parenting. People rarely agree.

Sometimes moms use that line as a crutch or to justify the way they do things because they are worried people are judging them. So, true statement, but a nerdy one.

The Marathon That Is Motherhood

Okay, my NYM buddy, it's time for a little chat. This isn't the best analogy ever, but we'll go with it. It's the best thing I can come up with to try to show a not-yet mom how a mom feels when you offer her parenting advice or criticize her parenting skills or decisions.

Let's say, my NYM friend, that you've been training for a year to run a marathon. You've done several half marathons, but you're ready for the big dog. You've been working your tail off, and your day has finally arrived.

The gun goes off, and the 26-mile course looms in front of you. You do great for the first eight miles, drag for two, get your second wind, and cruise for six. Then you get a vicious cramp in your side and down your leg, but you fight it through miles 17, 18, 19, and 20. Then the nausea kicks in, you stop to hurl, and your cramps get worse, but you keep going.

By mile 23, you just know you're going to die. You want so badly to finish the race, but you just can't. You have pains where you didn't know you had parts. At this point, you'd welcome the relief death would bring.

After 23.6 miles, you call it quits. Tears streaming down your cheeks, you fall down on the ground, rip off your number, and bury your face in your hands.

Then you hear someone calling your name. You look up. It's one of your girlfriends. She walks over from her spot as a spectator, kneels down, and pats you on the shoulder. She's just in time! Oh, how you could use some comfort and sympathy right now!

"Girl, what's the matter with you?" she says. "Why in the world did you quit?"

You look at her blankly. Does she think this qualifies as encouragement?

"This has been your dream for so long," she says, shaking her head in disappointment. "It's such a shame you couldn't make it just 2.6 more little miles. You know, if you wouldn't have drunk so much water at that first stop, you'd probably still be going. There are so many things you could have done to prevent this. I thought you always told me to run through the pain!"

You stare at your "friend," who has never run a marathon in her life. "How can you say that to me? You have no idea what I've been through. You've never run a marathon in your life!"

"No," she says, "but I know how to. I subscribe to *Runner's World,* you know. I've read every article in every issue for three years. Plus, I ran cross-country in high school, and I've run the Turkey Trot 10K every November for the past five years. My brothers have all run marathons. I watch them all the time. When I get out of med school, I'm going to start training and run the Boston Marathon. I love Boston! I'm going to run five marathons a year—at least. And when *I* start running marathons, I am *never* going to wimp out like you did— especially that close to the finish line. What a waste!"

If you can put yourself in that runner's shoes and imagine the emotions coursing through your head and heart at that moment, you can understand what a mom feels like when one of your parenting comments seems critical to her.

So if you aren't yet a mom, try your hardest not to offer unsolicited advice to moms. Even if you mean well, we're extra sensitive. And truthfully, motherhood is one case when the ideal isn't always practical, when our head knowledge just doesn't play out quite so smoothly in our real lives. My friend Melissa has learned this.

> I was arrogant in many ways about how one should parent. I would say that I knew I wouldn't do it perfectly, but I think I had myself set up believing that in reality, I really would do everything the right way. Now, looking back, I realize that I still have the same ideas about right ways to do certain things, but two things are different.
>
> One is that rules about raising kids aren't always as black-and-white as I thought. The second is that even if there is a right way to handle a situation, knowing it and actually doing it are two different things, and the latter is often more difficult than I understood. I forgot to factor in the will of my child. As much as I want to teach and train, the other person in the equation isn't always a willing recipient of that.

Your idea or suggestion for your mom-friend is probably fabulous. And in our heads, we usually know it to be wise and true (in theory), but we're really struggling at doing everything right all at once.

Doing the right thing is easier when you've had more than four hours of sleep in the last three weeks. Crazy, crazy things happen when you've been on mothering call 24/7 for months on end. Theories fly out the window. You switch to survival mode.

You're stepping into a deadly trap when you start telling moms how to raise their kids. More often than not, your words will come back to bite you in the buns.

The Bible actually speaks to this in Proverbs 27:1 (MSG): "Don't brashly announce what you're going to do tomorrow; you don't know the first thing about tomorrow."

So just hold your tongue, pray for your friend, and wait until God blesses you with children. Your words of wisdom might not change at all—but if they do, you'll be so glad you waited.

We moms just need some grace, some encouragement. We need our not-yet-mom friends to acknowledge that motherhood is a marathon and to love us unconditionally along the course.

Take the High Road, Mom

And if you're a mom, let's agree to drop the phrase "someday you'll understand" (and all variations of it!) altogether. You may have been offended by someone's usually true (but cutting) remark, but that doesn't mean you're allowed to throw back one of your own.

Those are words that wound, coming from someone who feels wounded. As the saying goes, hurt people *hurt* people. And that's never okay.

When a not-yet mom drops a hint or flat-out tells you you're doing something wrong, swallow your pride, bite your tongue (without saying that's what you're doing!) and just trust that someday, she will understand. You don't need to be the one to tell her so. When she does have kids, she'll still love you because you knew what her life would be like but didn't rub it in her face.

I'm a firm believer in speaking the truth—but only in love. The "someday you'll understand" line is true. But it's not often spoken in love. And it *is* very often abused.

Of course, no one can possibly fully understand motherhood until she's experienced it firsthand. I used to be a not-yet mom. Now I'm a mom. I had no idea motherhood would be this hard. I have yet to meet a mom who didn't think parenting was easier before she had kids (unless she has a live-in nanny and housekeeper).

So, yeah, the statement is true, and I can't back down on that fact.

But, hello, since when do we have to state everything that is true? She's fat. His nose is huge. Her teeth are crooked. His breath smells like poop. Her mother was a hooker. These statements may all be true, but we don't need to say them!

And if we really need to tell someone something, surely we can find a way to say it kindly.

"Someday you'll understand" doesn't really need to be said, and it certainly doesn't need to be said to hurt or exclude someone or to avenge yourself when you think you've been wronged. And besides, you can't know how the not-yet mom will respond in any given situation when she *does* become a mom.

"When you're a mom, you'll buy a mini-van. Just wait and see."

"You'll change your mind about having five children."

"You'll be begging for the epidural—trust me!"

"You'll give your children candy to stop a temper tantrum—even if you say you won't!"

Some of these may end up coming true. Some may not. None of them are necessary.

Let's Feel the Love

One of Paul's biggest themes in the New Testament was encouraging other believers to quit their nit-picking and cat fighting and just get along.

"So tend to your knitting," he said. "You've got your hands full just taking care of your own life before God. Forget about deciding what's right for each other. Here's what you need to be concerned about: that you don't get in the way of someone else, making life more difficult than it already is…So let's agree to use all our energy in getting along with each other. Help others with encouraging words; don't drag them down by finding fault" (Romans 14:12-13,19 MSG).

James has some similar words to share. "You can develop a healthy, robust community that lives right with God and enjoy its results only if you do the hard work of getting along with each other, treating each other with dignity and honor" (James 3:18 MSG).

What do you say we cut the conflict and get busy cultivating community? Let's start treating each other with all sorts of dignity and honor, like the Christ followers we claim to be.

You're
the Mom!

9

That Mommy Groove

Wouldn't life be wonderful if we all sailed smoothly into our mommy role and handled every situation with poise and grace? If our lives played out in real life the way they appeared in daydreams of old?

You know the dreams I'm talking about. Sunlight streaming through the window, mama and baby dressed in crisp, soft, white linen. Your adorable porcelain infant smiling up at you and cooing with recognition.

Your little tow-headed toddler wrapping you in the tightest bear hug his little arms can manage, cupping your face with his chubby little hands and kissing you full and hard on the lips.

Your curly-haired little girl chasing butterflies barefoot in a white eyelet dress, cheeks flushed with excitement, tiny wildflowers intertwined in her tousled locks.

Your little man kicking a soccer ball around the yard with his daddy, your two men in matching T-shirts—one big, one small—your son's little legs trying their best to keep up. You lounging on the deck, sipping lemonade, taking it all in.

If your life on a daily basis is slightly less serene than that, it's okay. Those moments will come, never fear, but they'll be fleeting. Be watching for them, or you could miss them. And in the meantime, enjoy the messier, crazier moments in your day. That's the stuff life is made of.

In our minds, most other moms' lives are always like the catalog spread. They are much more adequate at mothering. They're juggling everything we are and more, yet they don't seem fazed. They still show up at church with great clothes and makeup, and their Gappy babies don't have a hair out of place.

You can only assume that their little ones are healthy and happy, developing right on schedule. That their husbands are beyond satisfied in the bedroom. That they've found the key to balancing family, work, church, and pleasure. And that they're lovin' every minute of life as a mom.

Are you the only one who's having a rough go of it? Is there any hope that you'll get it together in the near future? Will you ever find your groove? Do you even know what one looks like?

I'd love to be able to tell you, "Just read this chapter, and you'll know all there is to know about being a super groovy mom!"

Okay, so maybe the title is the teensiest bit misleading. It hints at glowing examples from my life as a mom, practical tips I've gleaned on how to do motherhood right. How to quickly find that mommy groove and be the best mom you can be.

There's just one small glitch. Seven years into motherhood, and I've yet to find my groove. Oh sure, many parts are easier than they were when I first started. Some of the really tough stuff is forever in my past. But each new day seems to bring new challenges I'm not prepared for, brand-new opportunities for me to make a mess of everything.

So Tell Me What You Want, What You Really, Really Want

"You said you'd never write a book on parenting," my friend Amelia reminded me a few months ago.

"Did I say that?"

Of course I said it, and at the time, I certainly meant it. Motherhood is way too subjective. A book on parenthood creates endless opportunities to tick people off. I can see the picket lines now. I'm not thick-skinned enough to deal with all the hate mail, let alone riots in my front yard. I could have written a parenting book before I had kids, but not now!

I can write comfortably about marriage. No problem. For followers of Christ, the "rules of engagement" are much more straightforward. The Bible gives us wives lots of clear guidelines. Love your husband, respect him, be submissive, make passionate love at least three times a week. (What? That's not in your version?)

I can even write about sex. Just take a deep breath and don't think about the people you know who will be reading the book.

But parenting? There is definitely instruction in God's Word on the spiritual nurturing of your children, but the specifics of child rearing are conspicuously missing. I scoured the whole Bible and found a whole lot of nothin' about potty training, co-sleeping, or curbing temper tantrums in the middle of Target.

With such a sensitive, subjective topic, things could get very sticky very quickly. But my fear of making people mad wasn't the half of it. I didn't want to be a hypocrite. Why should I be handing out mothering advice (*selling* it, actually) when I couldn't go two hours as a mom without making a mistake? It seemed almost unethical.

I knew I couldn't give mothering advice to others when I was such a screwup myself. The day I got it together would be the day I wrote a parenting book. I have a hard enough time living up to what I've written in my marriage books. A book about being a mom would surely come back to bite me in the booty!

But then I realized something. As long as I don't claim to have it all together, I can still weave together some words of encouragement for moms. I'll start with moms who have just gotten started down Mommy Road. I can do baby's first year. I've survived three of them. And if I survive writing about *that,* I can move on from there.

And when I asked moms what they'd want to read in a book like this, their answers assured me that I might just be the woman for the job after all.

"I want to read about moms who are going through the same things I am."

"Funny stories."

"Honest struggles other parents go through so I don't feel so rotten."

"The honest truth in a humorous way."

"The real struggles all parents face."

"Other moms' experiences, trials, and victories."

"That not everyone is perfect."

"People messing up—so I know I'm normal when I feel like an idiot as a parent."

"Encouragement from knowing I'm not alone on this journey."

"That flying by the seat of your pants is a legitimate parenting tactic."

Aside from my cheeky friend Gail, who requested "a definitive guide on how to do everything right," I felt encouraged by what moms wanted to read. Can I do this? Yes I can!

In my brief writing career, I've found that roughly 98 percent of what resonates with women most in my books and blog are the accounts of my ineptitude (and sadly, I never lack self-deprecating anecdotes to share). It's human nature to be comforted by the fact that someone out there is more incompetent and inclined to screw up than you. So let me indulge you with some random tales of how *not* to find your mommy groove. By the end of this chapter, you should be flyin' high, thinking, *Man, I'm a good mom!* Your self-esteem will reach new heights. Glad I could be of assistance.

Chicken Little

I flipped on the baby monitor and crawled into bed at 1:00 a.m., dead tired. Thankfully, three-month-old Nina didn't make a peep until three hours later. It was 4:00 a.m. when I first heard her peep. Literally. She sounded like a baby chick.

What in the world? I jumped out of bed to see if she was gagging or something. Nope. She looked perfectly peaceful. Back to bed.

A minute later—chirp, chirp. Then eek, eek. Okay, so now she sounded like a chicken *and* a mouse.

Back to her room. Nothing. *Huh?* Back to our room. Then she started crying—a very weird cry. Ran to her room. It wasn't her. It must be Livi or Ava? But no. They were fine.

I went back to Nina's room, and I heard crying coming from *our* room. Ran back and forth between rooms. Someone was crying on our baby monitor, and it was *none* of our babies.

Then I heard, "Should we take him to the doctor?"

What? Then, *oh!* Our neighbors across the street had a seven-month-old son. Could it be…?

I checked Nina's monitor. Channel A. I checked *our* monitor. Channel D. Hmmm…Switched ours to channel A. Two seconds later, I heard…breathe in, breathe out, breathe in…My baby. Go figure.

"We could listen to them some more," Gabe said. He was kidding. I think.

Smacked Upside the Head

At 2:30 a.m., I warmed a bottle for a crying, teething ten-month-old by the light of the microwave. (Please—no comments about tooth decay as a result of late-night bottles, the necessity of letting babies cry themselves to sleep, the benefits of breast-feeding for at least 12 months, or the hazards of using the microwave to heat bottles. I'm having a hard enough time as it is, thanks.)

Water heated, bottle mixed, cap screwed on, I shut the microwave door and headed quickly toward the darkened stairs and my screaming child, when SMACK. *Have I ever felt this much pain?* Nothing came to mind.

I thought I knew my kitchen like the back of my hand, but I misjudged the length of the dividing wall between the refrigerator and the stairs landing. I hit the wall straight on, face-first. HARD. I thought for sure my forehead had shattered in a million pieces, which were settling in atop my cheek bones, held inside my head by the skin on my face.

I stumbled up the stairs in a daze, my head throbbing. I immediately felt a nice goose-egg above my left eye, which was still there 24 hours later, as was my headache. Mama always said there was a reason my middle name wasn't Grace.

Share Your Story

Writing down our life experiences is somehow very therapeutic. And in the twenty-first century, one simple way to share those stories with others is to start a blog. I can't tell you how many moms have told me what a great outlet blogging has been for them. It validates their mom-hood, gives them a voice they wouldn't otherwise have, and puts them in contact with other moms experiencing the same things.

When something awful or hard or crazy happens, it's so great to be able to instantly share your tale on the web and glean some much-needed empathy and pats on the back from your readers the world over.

When my youngest daughter was about three weeks old, I blogged a bit about my postpartum "bliss."

> Motherhood is a breeze. Having three children is easier than I ever dreamed. I'm not sure what I thought would be so difficult about it. Surely not being up all night nursing an infant while your middle child fights a fever and stomachache, and you yourself are stricken with violent diarrhea. "Sorry you've only been nursing for 20 seconds, Nina, but Mommy has to poop, and NOW."

> Surely not going out on a date to a Mexican restaurant with just your husband and newborn and eating the world's greasiest chicken taco with your right hand and holding a fussy baby in your left. Nina's favorite pink blanket will remain forever stained.

Surely not writing just seven sentences on your blog and then having to get out of your chair to comfort the crying baby that you just spent 20 minutes getting to sleep. I'm back!

Surely not spending the entire 3:00 a.m. hour trying your darnedest to get your gassy baby to burp. Who says people can't survive on three hours of sleep for infinite nights in a row? I'm doing just fine, see?

Surely not changing your baby on the floor, making sure to put a diaper under her in case she pees, and being the target of an explosive projectile liquid poop, not unsimilar to a horizontal erupting volcano. Picture a squeeze bottle of mustard lying on its side, open. A big man takes a running leap and lands on the mustard bottle. That's how big and fast and yellow it was. Gabe has pictures.

And sadly, I cannot remember one single more event that transpired in the last month. I cannot remember anything at all. Not my children's names. Not simple vocabulary words. Not the time of day or what I opened the refrigerator for. I only pray that my loss of brain functioning is temporary.

Complain with Caution

I've already mentioned that illusive balance between being real and being a complainer. As followers of Christ, I think we have to carefully weigh our words before we say or write them.

I want so badly to share the real me with others—my heart, my struggles, my pain, my joys. And it can be tough to know when I've gone beyond being honest about the tough times and started moaning and groaning about my lot in life.

I want to be counted among those who are gut-honest about their parenting struggles but who love their little ones with everything in them. Who constantly check their attitudes to make sure they're clean and fresh—not reeking of whining or complaining.

We've got to find a way to let people know how hard this is (or do we really?) without sounding as if we've been cursed. Our children are among life's hugest blessings. We *must* not talk about them like they've ruined our perfect lives.

And how would you like someone talking about *you* as if you were their biggest, most annoying burden? Maybe someone did (a parent?) and still is. I'm so sorry about that, but can we break the cycle?

You know how it is when you're sick with the flu or a sinus infection or just have bad menstrual cramps. You're afraid that if you don't moan and groan and complain about your pain every ten minutes, your boss (or coworker or husband or friend or mom) is going to think you're *fine*. And what's even worse than feeling absolutely lousy? Feeling absolutely lousy without any sympathy!

Plus, we certainly don't want to give the false impression that our lives are perfect and easy. We want other moms to like us, so we need to make sure we complain as much as they do.

We need to draw a fine line. Can we creatively find a way to encourage other moms by honestly sharing our hardships but by also reinforcing the idea that our children are a blessing from God? Can we share our struggles without wallowing in them? Can we voice our concerns and troubles but then actually take steps to *do* something about them?

When I'm speaking to women's groups about marriage, I call women (myself included) on the carpet about this very thing. So many of them want to rail and harp on their husbands, but they don't actually want to take any steps to improve their marriages. The yipping and griping is too much fun.

When we're chatting with other moms, can we bring things back to Scripture? Let's focus on simple truths like "The joy of the Lord is my strength" and "I can do all things through Christ who strengthens me."

I'm so encouraged by women (and I know so many!) who are transparent and candid but always bring everything back to Christ.

Have I Shown You Her Two-Month Pictures?

So let's talk about blogging for a little bit. There aren't really any rules for blogging about your baby. Oh sure, some people don't like the words "pee" and "poop" and whatnot, but who has time to invent cozy little alternative terms for body waste?

I'm going to tell you something that your closest friends are afraid to say to you. There is a delicate balance between sharing information about your child and sharing *too much* information (TMI) about your child. The sooner you find that balance, the happier we'll all be.

We've all met people in the TMI club. You yourself may be a charter member. I'll admit, you can find me hanging out in the club- house every so often. (To my credit, when I first became a mom, I was *much* worse.)

It gets old right quick when every word out of a woman's mouth is about her child. This might be hard for you to believe, but as extraor- dinary as your child may seem to you, she's just really not all that amazing to the rest of us.

To your parents, probably. To your sisters, possibly. But to everyone else? Not so much. Sadly, we really don't care about half the stuff your baby or child does unless it's truly spectacular or unbelievably heinous or uncommonly sweet or just plain funny.

You've got to use a filter though. If we see every single picture and hear every single latest greatest thing he does, we're going to start tuning you out. Share just the brightest, best, worst, and funniest things he does. Pick your three favorite pictures out of the 300 you just took.

I know that a lot of people blog primarily for long-distance grand- parents, but still. I remember my dad looking through our photo albums of our firstborn when she was just a baby. "Where are all the other people?" he asked. "All these pictures look exactly the same." And this is coming from a grandparent. Granted, a male grandparent, but even so.

I recall being mildly offended, but I knew he was right. Two hundred pictures of your one-month-old—even if she's wearing 200 different outfits? Snore.

My cousins Kyla and Kelly love the word "snore." It can be used for all sorts of occasions, but mostly when someone is talking about something she alone finds fascinating.

Twenty pictures of your little girl's first bite of carrots? Snore. Thirty pictures of baby boy's first tooth? Snore.

Trust me—you'll be a much more balanced (and interesting) person if you talk (and blog) about a variety of topics. I try to keep that in mind while writing. Do my readers want to hear about every move Nina makes? Or would they enjoy words that focus on *them*, the readers? Words and stories that offer them the opportunity to think, laugh, and ponder their own lives?

And if you just can't muster up any think-and-ponder fodder, then just go for the laughs. That's what we all secretly want the most anyway. Bring on the funny!

And honestly, there's another reason we're annoyed by the doting, gushing parents who can't stop talking about their baby. We secretly hate that they think *their* child is the best thing since Dippin' Dots. We can only assume that they think their child is cuter and more brilliant than ours, and that's obviously not the case.

Boasting Is for the Birds

We can all appreciate the miracle that is your child, but we'd prefer to do it on our own. When you tell us (demand, really) to admire every single thing about your amazing, one-of-a-kind progeny, the miracle tends to lose its appeal for most of us.

Believe it or not, we don't actually need you to tell us that your child is in the ninety-ninth percentile for height. We're smart folks. We can do a quick perusal of a room, size everyone up, and surmise that your kid is pretty tall.

We also don't need to know every single feat (and I use the term loosely) that your child has accomplished. Sharing is okay; bragging is not. And be selective. Please. Believe it or not, there are very few child prodigies out there. Yours probably isn't one of them.

I know how hard it can be to stuff that pride down. I remember taking our youngest daughter for her six-month checkup. Shots aside, I do love a good well-baby visit. For a small co-pay, you get to sit there and listen to a professional doctor ooh and ahh over your astounding offspring.

I always find myself in the midst of a paradox of sorts. I eat up the compliments, but I'm so annoyed by mothers who think their babies are somehow superior to all the other babies in the world just because they rolled over first or got a tooth first or are in that ridiculous ninety-ninth percentile.

So the nurse weighed Nina. Nineteen pounds, 13 ounces. So far, so good. I felt that percentile pride start to kick in. You know, where you're proud of your breast milk and how chubby it has made your baby.

Then she measured her. Twenty-six inches. Not good. She didn't even stretch her leg out. I was just positive she was longer than that. She *had* to be.

The nurse leaves. I tell myself to let it slide. *No biggie, Marla. This will be good practice for you in stuffing your pride down where it belongs.*

I can't do it. I open a drawer, find the tape measure and a pen, and measure her myself. Yeah, I took calculus in high school. Better yet, I aced Math for Elementary Teachers in college.

Twenty-nine inches. I knew it!

The doctor came in and read her chart. "Looks like she's in the ninety-seventh percentile for weight and the fifty-seventh percentile for height."

Trying not to sound exactly like the kind of mother that exasperates me (yet somehow unable to help it), I ask if maybe she could remeasure her.

She does and comes up with 29.75 inches. Aha! Off the chart.

We're talking one hundred fifth percentile, if there were such a thing. I felt a quick surge of self-satisfaction.

Then I felt like a total loser. This pride struggle is one of the reasons I didn't feel up to the task of writing a parenting book. Bear with me as we work through it together.

Oops! I Did It Again!

I asked some of my friends to share some blunders from the first year of motherhood so I wouldn't feel as if I were the only one with issues.

They did not disappoint.

"About a month ago, my husband was changing our baby boy's diaper," says one friend who prefers to remain incognito for this particularly sensitive tale. "He called me in the room to show me that the tip of poor baby's little boy parts (okay, penis—it's hard to say that word!) was swollen and red. Poor kid.

"Hubby asked me if I'd been pulling the skin back and wiping things down really well. What in the world? No. I got a quick man-tutorial in keeping things clean. I had no idea. I've never been a boy, you know! I thought since he was circumcised, we were good to go! I put him in the tub, let him soak for a little while, and washed him down, and he was as good as new."

I decided to give her one more chance to let me use her name. "Ha!" she said. "I can imagine my son picking up this book at 15, horrified and yelling, 'Mo-om!'"

My friend Terri's stories were G-rated, so she was fine using names. Here are some important parenting tips she learned the hard way by the time her boys were one.

> 1. John was a month old before it occurred to me that I should uncurl his little fists and wash his hands. He had dust balls the size of Chicago.

> 2. John wore cloth diapers with plastic pants over them. If you forget the plastic pants, your lap will be very soggy by the end of church.

3. Toddlers left to play on the (enclosed) front porch will eat ants. Ants do NOT scrape easily off toddler tongues.

4. Do not place your child's playpen close to the aquarium. Matthew stood on toys so he could reach the edge of the aquarium and pull it down into his playpen—on top of his legs. Luckily, all we ended up with was a drenched baby (with bruised legs and *lots* of floppy fish and gravel in the playpen).

"All I know," says Terri, now a grandmother, "is that God takes care of fools and children."

"When my son was four months old," one friend told me, "we were visiting my in-laws in another state. We all went to Costco and were just walking around when suddenly I realized the cart with my little guy in it was missing. I guess I just assumed someone else in the family was pushing it. Not so. We all quickly backtracked and found him right where I left him, in the book section. (I'm bawling right now remembering.) A sweet lady was crooning to him that it would be okay, she'd find his mommy. She had sent her own little boy to customer service to make an announcement to find us. I felt horrid. I still do."

"When my son was a year old," said another friend, "I left him downstairs while I ran up to get a diaper because he had filled his pants. Moments later, I found him eating dirt. Lovely. I assumed he had gotten into one of my houseplants. Two seconds later, my nose told me it was not dirt. He had eaten 80 percent of the contents of his diaper and smeared the rest all over himself. I had to soak Q-tips in warm water to get it out of his ears and nostrils."

I am thrilled that (so far!) my kids have stuck to a feces-free diet, but the poo-ingesting is more common than you might think.

Another friend shares, "We've had poop eating (and feeding to baby sister), dirt eating, little boys getting knocked into coffee tables and needing stitches as mom is just getting out of the shower (PBS Kids let me down that morning), babies crying and crying while mom is trying to console another one or make supper, mom throwing a nursing baby in the air and flashing a roomful of people because she mistook her baby's hand on her stomach to be a mouse running across her...I could go on and on."

My mom-in-law shared about the time she locked her keys in the car sometime before Gabe turned one. "Being a young, first-time mom," she says, "I just didn't think to make sure to get Gabe out with me. Our car was parked on the main street of a little town. It was hot out, and there he sat in his car seat. I had no phone and no way of asking for help because I didn't want to leave the car with him in it. He was old enough to give me a look that said, "This is great," so unaware of what was going on. He was fine, but I was frantic. Finally, someone came along and called the cops. An officer came with one of those flat bars that go down the side of your door and unlatched the lock."

I can't count the number of moms who shared car-seat-scare stories. You inadvertently leave one or more of the five points unharnessed. The seat belt holding the car seat in place somehow came unfastened. The infant carrier isn't snapped onto the base. You keep pulling over to the side of the road to adjust baby's tiny head, which is always flopping off to one side.

One dear friend summed up this universal mom-oops beautifully. "You know how they fall asleep when you're out and about, so you put them in their car seat but don't fasten it? And then you end up putting them back in the car and still have not fastened it and never even realize it until you take them out safely at home? I hope you can't relate, because if you can, you've felt like a *lousy* mother. But then you just have to remember that 30 years ago we didn't even have car seats, and we rode all over the place in cars. Somehow some of us still survived."

Guardian angels, that's what I say. "For he will command his angels concerning you to guard you in all your ways; they will lift you up in their hands, so that you will not strike your foot against a stone" (Psalm 91:11-12).

Obviously, we have to watch our little ones as closely as we can, but sometimes things happen. Like babies rolling down the stairs or getting dropped or Mama leaning down to get them out of their infant seat and banging their little head on the underside of a counter. Or carrying them up the stairs and tripping and falling. Or carrying them down the stairs and slipping and falling.

Praise the Lord for His angels!

How Do Those Words Taste?

None of us go into motherhood planning to leave car seats unfastened or drop our babies or let our little guys' private parts get infected. We don't plan to have trouble breast-feeding or plan to have children who throw tantrums or eat ants.

But this doesn't mean that we'll escape these and similar undesirable mothering scenarios. That's why I tell not-yet moms to be careful what they boast about. Just as you don't want your little one eating poop, you don't want to end up eating your words.

Trust me—things will not always go according to your well-laid parenting plans.

"I read a lot of books on how to do everything from bathing your newborn to the best way to discipline," said one woman. "Our first-born did not read these books and did not realize how things were supposed to go. I thought that if you learned what you needed and you applied it accordingly, everything would be fine. Now I know you learn as you go, you do what works, and if it fails, you try something else. Most of all, you go to the Creator of your child and ask Him what to do."

"Well, of course, I thought that no matter what, I was going to be the perfect parent," one woman told me. "I wouldn't make the same mistakes as my parents. I was going to be patient, not yell or spoil my children. They would be well-behaved and polite, never throw tantrums in public, and on and on. Whenever I saw some trait in another parent that I thought was wrong or ignorant, I would think to myself, *I would never do or say that to my child.* While there are some things

I've stuck with, there are others (like not yelling or losing my cool) that have flown right out the window when I've heard my daughter whine and scream for an hour straight. I then get down off my high horse and realize most moms out there are doing the best they can."

"I really thought that as long as I did certain things, the children would automatically respond in a certain way," says Tracy. "I have realized kids don't work like that—they have a mind of their own!"

"Ha!" says Cherith. "I had it all figured out before I had kids. I don't have a clue now. I think the biggest lesson I've learned is that even though I thought I knew exactly what I would do in every situation, I don't really know what I will do until it happens. I have to remember that when I am talking to people who are going through something I haven't gotten to yet. Also, just because something worked for one of my kids doesn't mean it will work for another one or for someone else's kid. I think I've learned not to think of myself as an expert on anything."

I love what Cherith said about being careful when she talks to someone who is going through something she hasn't gotten to yet.

Remember that "someday you'll understand" line that moms throw out to NYMs? It might comfort NYMs to know that they aren't the only recipients of this classic one-liner. It's also used by moms of older kids when talking to moms of younger kids. And moms of two or more children say it to moms of one child.

Something happens after our first child hits the six-month mark or so. We *do* get into a semblance of a groove, life gets easier again, and we're tempted to fall back into critic mode. And we begin to make promises we just may not be able to keep. *When I have two children, I'm going to maintain my current lifestyle. I've been through this baby thing before and passed with flying colors. This next time through will be a breeze! No sweat.*

Or let's say you're a mom to a two-year-old and a baby. You're silently observing a mom and her six-year-old boy. *When* my *son is six, he's certainly not going to act like* that! you say to yourself. *If that mom would have disciplined her son at two (like I am with my son), he wouldn't be acting like that four years later.*

I have a rule (it's one you might want to adopt): Don't judge a mom until you've walked in her shoes.

Let me clarify. I have three children. All girls. As I write this, they are seven, five, and two. I really shouldn't judge anyone at all, but I *especially* don't judge moms who have (1) more children than me, (2) boys, and (3) children older than mine.

I've bitten holes in my poor tongue when women without children tell me how they will parent differently (and better) than me someday. And it's just as bad (if not worse) when a mom of an infant says something like, "When *my* child is three, he will not _____." (You fill in the blank.)

I may not like how someone's ten-year-old daughter is acting, but my lips will stay zipped until my oldest safely reaches eleven (make that fourteen, just to be safe) without incident.

And past experience says this won't happen. Better to swallow my words before they ever come out of my mouth than to publicly eat them somewhere down the road.

Take It to the Bank

I do feel a little badly that this book isn't oozing with practical tips to make your mama life run more smoothly. So let me share a few pieces of advice I received once from some wise old souls.

I was pregnant with my first baby and substitute teaching a group of fourth graders. They were done with their work and getting restless, so I had them take out a piece of paper and a pencil.

"Write down your best piece of parenting advice for me," I told them. "What is the one thing you think I should know before I become a mother?"

I'm so glad I asked for their wisdom. Who knows where I would be today without it? Most of them are cute, but some made me a little sad, knowing that they must have gotten these ideas of parenthood from their own moms and dads. Here's a sampling:

"Babies cry a lot, so buy earmuffs!"

"Don't have more than two kids. They'll ruin your life!"

"Feed him enough but not too much."

"Name him Fred. Then you can say, 'Come here, Fred!'"

"Beware! You may be up all night caring for your baby."

"Watch out for how much money you spend on them, or there goes your money!"

"Babies are loud. Consider earplugs."

"Be prepared for smells you don't smell every day."

"Kids hate it when you call them by their full name."

"Never have too many kids. They will overwhelm you."

"Feed the baby daily."

"Don't do diapers. Leave that to your husband."

And that's about all you need to know to be the world's best mother. Remember, you're going to goof up, mess up, screw up. But don't beat yourself up. Get up, dust off yourself (and your baby), wipe up the poop, and move on with your life.

Our little ones are resilient and forgiving. Our God is a God of grace. These experiences keep us humble and remind us of our need for a Savior. And those angels are always on duty.

10

Changing Your World

No matter how much we love being moms, we all have something outside of motherhood that ignites passion within us as well. For me, it's writing. And reading. And photography. And encouraging people. And making small bits of money stretch really, really far.

Think back a few (or many) years to your childhood. What did you love? What were you passionate about? How did you spend your time? What gave you joy long before peer pressure was a factor?

A child is the rawest, purest form of a person. Sadly, the world quickly gets ahold of us, drains the joy out of us, and molds us into who we "should" be. We start out uninhibited and free. We do what we like, we voice our honest opinions, we embrace the world with open arms.

Of course we need to be taught and trained to do what's right. Left to our own devices, we'd never choose to follow Christ, to obey, to be unselfish, or to love others.

But I'm not talking about that. I'm talking about our gifts, talents, passions, desires. I'm talking about that innate love for animals or books or cars or baking or painting or whatever God planted deep inside our souls when He first created us. I'm talking about something we're uniquely gifted at—something God can use to bring lost souls to Himself.

What did I love when I was little? You already know I loved taking care of my baby dolls. I wanted to be a mommy.

I also loved to read. I read hundreds, no, *thousands* of books as a child. And I loved to write. I loved paper, pencils, books. I loved words—speaking them and listening to them, yes, but mostly reading and writing them.

I wanted to be a librarian. When I was ten, I made a card catalog of my books, taped labels on their spines, and shelved them in alphabetical order. I invited friends and family to check out books from my personal library.

I wanted to be a writer. I scrawled poems on scraps of paper starting in first grade. I was constantly making books—notebook pages stapled together, pictures cut from old JCPenney catalogs and glued on the pages, stories written beside the pictures.

My parents never discouraged me from pursuing what I loved.

Not everything I loved was a sign of the future. I loved baseball—listened to every Cincinnati Reds game on the radio and kept score. I loved playing bakery and decorating mud cakes. I loved creating obstacle courses for my siblings and cousins in our big country yard. None of those really interest me today, but they still helped make me who I am.

Think of your childhood dreams. Put on your reminiscing cap, and remember what you loved. *That's* what you want to do—in the purest sense. Now hold that thought.

Is It Okay to Dream?

"Follow your heart!"

"Chase after your dreams!"

"Be whoever you want to be!"

You've heard all these slogans before. What do you think—are they unrealistic? A bit self-centered? Too much hoopla for a woman serious about her mothering responsibilities?

Maybe, maybe not.

I recently attended a Women of Faith conference, where the theme was "Amazing Freedom." Many of the speakers encouraged us to live our dreams.

One of my friends told me she enjoyed the conference but found all the talk about dreaming to be a bit over the top. "God doesn't promise we can go out and do anything we fancy," she said. "Sometimes what He has planned for us is not what we had in mind. He puts dreams on hold. He has responsibilities and obligations for us that we must meet. That's real life."

I agree with her. And I don't.

Yes, our dreams get put on hold sometimes.

No, God never promises to grant us our every fantasy.

And no, your dreams can't be all about you. Especially if you're a wife and mom. Leaving your family members to fend for themselves while you go find yourself and pursue your life calling is not an option.

But on the other hand, I think we tend to underestimate God. Many times we just suck it up and unselfishly put our dreams and passions aside because we think that's best for the kingdom.

Have we considered the possibility that God just might let us have our cake and eat it too? That maybe He has a place for us right inside His kingdom that has room for us to be wives and moms while doing something we're passionate about? Something we can do that will matter for eternity?

Our dreams don't have to be all about us, but they don't have to be exclusively about our kids either. I actually think our kids are better off if we have dreams and passions outside of them. They feel less pressure when they see that Mommy and Daddy (and the rest of the world) don't orbit around them. And a child respects a mother who uses her talents in some way or pursues a dream outside of motherhood.

I've read a lot of parenting books lately, and frankly, I'm sick to death of the oxygen mask analogy (you figure it out), but it's true. Motherhood is largely about self-sacrifice (as is following Christ in general), but if you neglect your own needs, you'll be less fit to meet your family's. The trouble is differentiating between needs and selfish wants.

My mom was a kindergarten teacher before she had kids, and she never went back to work. I remember (wrongly) wishing she had a "real" job besides being a mom. My friends' moms worked, and in my mind, that was awesome because they could afford more clothes and toys and better vacations.

My friends, on the other hand, would have given an arm and a leg for a mom who was available. A mom who put her kids before a job. And a family that played and prayed together. And parents who stayed together long after the kids grew up and left the house.

I do remember how proud I felt when my mom played the piano at church. Everyone was always so impressed with her talents—and that made me feel good.

We all want our kids to pursue their dreams. What better way to help them do that than to model it to them while they're growing up? *Mom follows her dreams and still loves spending time with us. I can do that someday too!*

God honors a woman who knows how to prioritize—God, hubby, kids, and then the other stuff. If we do it in that order, it will all be added to us (Matthew 6:33). Of course, maintaining and living out those priorities isn't always easy.

Family First

Let me make one thing clear. God's plan for your life never includes ministering to others while your own family's needs go unmet.

Sure, your children must learn the value of sacrifice. But that's different. I'm talking about my girls knowing in their heart of hearts that they are more important to me than any book or trip or conference or contract. That my greatest joy comes not from being an author or speaker or whatever, but from being Mrs. Gabe and their mommy.

And they cannot know this in their hearts unless I demonstrate it with my actions. Talk won't cut it. Words don't mean squat unless I back them up.

Following a dream requires more sacrifice from people who are raising children than from people without kids (or with grown-up ones). But you'll have to sacrifice your *own* stuff, not your kids'.

Sure, your kids can occasionally make sacrifices for your dream—frozen pizza instead of pot roast, helping out extra with chores, or whatever. But they shouldn't have to be sacrificing for you at every turn.

Here's how I look at it. My mom sacrificed for me. I sacrifice for my girls. My mom *and* my girls shouldn't all have to give up everything for *me*. What message does that send? Only this: that I am the most important person in the world!

We must never, ever sacrifice our kiddos on the altar of our dreams. We'll regret it forever and ever.

Yes, I dreamed of writing books one day, but I'm living out my absolute biggest dream of all right this very second. A husband and three beautiful daughters. My other dreams are big too, but they are secondary. And those dreams wouldn't be meaningful or even possible without my hubby and girls.

My Mom Always…

I was driving along this evening, on my way to pick up some pizza, and I got to thinking. What kinds of things will my girls remember about their childhood? Will they remember the games we played, the puzzles we put together, and the books we read? Or will they remember my writing deadlines and me shooing them away to watch a movie while I worked?

Will they remember helping me make pumpkin bread and chocolate chip cookies? Or will they remember eating McDonald's a lot because Mommy was too tired to make supper?

Will they remember our talks about Jesus and reading stories from the Bible? Or will they remember the times I lost my temper and yelled at them?

I want our home to be characterized by love and fun and learning and Jesus.

It's never too early—or too late!—to start making memories with your little one. I encourage you to write down some things you'd like your child to remember about you when he grows up. Check your list periodically and make sure you're on track to leave the best kind of memories you can.

I asked some women, "When your children are grown, what kinds of things do you want them to say and remember about you?"

"That their mommy was always praying and loved Jesus with her whole heart," says Jill. "That their mommy liked to have fun with them and loved to hear their laughs! That their mommy never wished a day away...every day was a treasure."

"I want them to want to be like me," Lindsey says. "I want them to think of me as a godly woman. I want them to want to be close to me and include me in their lives. I want them to remember all the times we had together and that I was always there for them."

"I want them to be able to say that their mom loved God with all her heart, all her soul, all her mind, all her strength," says Gail. "And that she obeyed Him. Always. That she showed them what faith looks like.'"

"I want them to say that I was a godly mom," says Jessica B. "That I showed them Christ and loved them unconditionally. I want them to say that I laughed a lot and goofed around a lot. I want them to say that they loved to hear me sing. (No one else in the world would say that!) I want them to say I adored and honored their father. And that they always caught us kissing."

"I want them to be able to say that I truly loved them and that I gave selflessly to provide for them," says Molly. "I want them to admire my commitment to the Lord and to aspire to follow in my footsteps. I'd also like them to say I was a source of wisdom and comfort and a provider of warmth and security. Finally, I'd like them to be able to say they enjoy my company."

"That I loved them, prayed with them, taught them about Jesus," says Anne Marie. "That I was silly and fun, helped other people, loved their daddy, valued people over things, was bold, loved Jesus, was a good friend."

"I want my son to remember that I enjoyed spending time with him," Shelly says, "that I paid attention when he spoke, that I loved Jesus and taught him to do the same, that I was never too busy to listen, that I cared about what was going on in his life, that I was involved in his activities but allowed him to spread his wings, that I taught him to do things for himself but was always there to help him if he needed it. That I loved his father and made our marriage a priority. That I was an example of what his future wife should be like."

"That I was beautiful and had a great body," says Krysty. "Just kidding!"

My Mama

I didn't know this until recently, but my mom always dreamed of having some type of ministry with my dad. Maybe a marriage ministry or a parenting ministry—speaking to women about loving their husbands and raising their children, sharing wisdom from her homeschooling experience.

That ministry never came to fruition—or so she thought.

Mom was too busy loving her own husband, caring (and praying) for her own four children. No time or opportunity materialized for that ministry she dreamed of. After two years of teaching kindergarten, she never went back into teaching or into the workforce at all.

She volunteered in countless ways at our church and blessed all sorts of people in all kinds of ways, but she never became involved in "full-time ministry."

Fast-forward many, many years. Her kids are all married, and she has six grandchildren so far. We kids are no longer 9, 6, 3, and a newborn. We're 32, 29, 26, and 23.

And one day, a thought hit her—and she shared that thought with me. God *did* have a full-time ministry for her all along—to raise four children who would ultimately be in full-time ministry themselves: an author, a youth pastor, and two youth pastors' wives.

Without her dedication to her family—her love, support, and time in prayer—who knows what career paths her children would have chosen? (Not that full-time ministry is the only way to serve Christ—it absolutely isn't!)

Mom made a huge sacrifice to give up her dream so her children could spend their adult lives serving the Lord. And looking back, she wouldn't have it any other way.

Just last week she e-mailed me a copy of a note I wrote her nine years ago. I only vaguely remember writing it.

> Dear Mom,
>
> This letter has two purposes: (1) to thank you for something special you did for me and (2) to make you cry. I was just reading *Women Leaving the Workplace* by Larry Burkett. It talks about how hundreds of women, most of whom had college degrees, left work to stay at home with their families—something I'm pretty sure I want to do. Anyway, one of the sections was kids writing in about how their mom staying at home impacted their lives. It made me remember how when I used to get mad, I'd always say, "If you would just get a job, we'd have enough money..." I'm SORRY for all the times I hurt you by saying that! In fact, I'm sorry for ALL the thousands of times I've hurt your feelings. Thinking about becoming a mother has caused me to feel haunted by my past, I guess. THANK YOU for staying home with me and homeschooling me and praying for me and loving me unconditionally. You mean the world to me.
>
> > I love you!
> > Marla
>
> P.S. Dry your eyes now.
>
> P.P.S. This one is for Dad. Daddy, thank you for being the best dad in the world to me. I love you like crazy. And I love you *because* you're crazy. You and Mom are my heroes. For real.

When you're 56 years old, looking back on your life thus far, what do you want to see? A career and ministry that is mostly behind you? Or the promise of years and years of service to God ahead of you in the form of your children and their spouses?

One of my mom's favorite verses is 3 John 4: "I have no greater joy than to hear that my children are walking in the truth."

I am so grateful to God that He has blessed me with the opportunity to serve Him in a capacity I love (writing and speaking) while I'm raising my daughters. But I have to guard my role as Mommy with my life.

I never want those precious little girls to resent the ministry because it took up all of Mommy's time and energy. I never want them to think to themselves, "I wish Mommy loved *me* as much as she loves to write."

If I'm honest, I'll admit that I'd give an arm and a leg for my daughters to join me in ministry in some way when they're grown. But I must be careful to pray for God's will for my girls, not just my own selfish agenda.

Lord, show me when and how you want me to sacrifice my own goals and dreams for my children's future in You. And thank You for the times You graciously allow me to have both.

Times Have Changed

"Things just aren't how they used to be. In this day and age, you need two salaries just to get by."

I hear this a lot. And I'm afraid I'm going to have to disagree.

Yes, if you want to keep up with the Belladuccis next door, you and your hubby will both need to work.

Believe it or not, you can actually survive without cable TV, new cars, the latest cell phones, eating out every weekend, and living in the most desirable subdivision.

When I was growing up, we didn't have a lot of money. I do remember feeling a twinge of something—envy?—each Christmas when my friends returned to school from break with completely new wardrobes and all the latest gadgets and toys. But then again, I also remember feeling a twinge of something—pity?—when many of my friends had parents they never saw, parents who got divorced, family situations that just plain stunk.

I had a happy childhood. And it had nothing to do with money. Gabe and I came from similar backgrounds, and he remembers being happy too.

My mom-in-law, Janelle, recently shared with me what it was like living on $14,000 a year for many, many years (which still wouldn't translate to much in 2008 dollars). How did they do it?

"We went on a camping vacation every year for 14 years. We drove old cars and kept them in good running order. We ate out at McDonalds for lunch on Fridays, and that was our eating out for the week. We ate meals that lasted for two days (like spaghetti). We only bought jeans, underwear, and socks new. We went to a lot of garage sales when the boys were little. We lived within our means—no credit cards.

"We enjoyed each other, so we could do very little and still have fun. Our friends were in the same boat, so there was no pressure to live a certain way. We didn't feel bad that we couldn't go out to eat because they couldn't either. Church events and sports were our hobbies—things that cost nothing. Church was huge to us, and we saved and saved so the boys could go to camp every summer.

"And the most important thing was to pray, stay close to God, to try to make Him Lord of our lives. He knew our every need and wanted us to be satisfied—and thrilled—when those needs were met. I was more content then with nothing than I am now."

Janelle stayed home until the boys were in school, and then she taught art and physical education at the Christian school they attended. Her hours allowed her to be home when they were home.

"I have always felt strongly that God gave us our children to raise, and therefore, we are to take that seriously and not give them to someone else. We want our values in them, not someone else's. We know our own children, and if Satan is trying to get at them, we would recognize it. A babysitter wouldn't. We can take them before God's throne.

"It's no different today. Rock made $6.00 an hour and was laid off during the winter. It's a choice to stay home. The pressure of society is just that. If we cave, then we cave. Maybe I'm too black-and-white. But if my sons and daughters-in-law can make it work with three kids apiece, then I'd say it can be done."

And there you have it. When you're afraid of stepping on toes over delicate issues like this one, just gently shove your mother-in-law up onto your soapbox and let her do your dirty work.

Jess's Story

While we're putting in-laws on soapboxes, I'm going to let my sister-in-law Jess take a turn on one. I briefly mentioned her story in chapter 7—married to Josh (my youth-pastor brother) with three gorgeous kids, she longed for a fulfilling career until God showed her how to find contentment in being a mommy. Here's the rest of her story:

> Somewhere between Ethan and Gavin, I got really frustrated with "just" being a stay-at-home mom. At the same time (God really has a sense of humor) I had to defend tooth and nail why we should let nursing women bring their babies to our women's retreat. They were saying that working women could come (their bottle-fed babies could stay with dad) but not nursing women because their babies would bother people.
>
> Yet the year before, I had brought three-month-old Ethan, and one of the most frequent comments in the "share time" was how much the older women loved being able to love on the younger women's babies.
>
> So I'm defending why we should support women staying home with their babies to this committee of older women while I myself was bemoaning the fact that I had to stay home with my babies. Ironic.
>
> Anyway, about halfway through this conflict, God started

poking my chest, saying, *Hypocrite! You don't even believe this!* And I thought, *You know, You're right.*

So at that point I started studying all the parts of the Bible about women and mothers. I got out my *Strong's Exhaustive Concordance* and looked up the Greek and everything. And God totally revealed to me that the home is the most important place for mothers to be.

At that point, He gave me a great peace and joy in being at home (tears are welling in my eyes even now because this was such a spiritual, emotional breakthrough for me). I could now view my job as a stay-at-home mom as something to rejoice in and something more fulfilling than the other things I thought I wanted.

When I look at other women who work and see how busy they are, I am so sad for them. When I work with teens who wish their moms were home when they had a really bad day at school, my heart breaks. Of course, I still have my "Oh, to have a 40-hour job" moments, but God has given me an immense passion for my "job" and His calling on my life.

And God has been so faithful to place tons of ministry opportunities in Jess's lap. Things she wouldn't have the time to do if she had a "real" job. He has provided for their family financially, freeing her up to use her gifts, talents, and time to make a difference in so many people's lives.

Get a load of these great things God has brought into her life. "I go to a women's prayer group (a homeschooled girl ministers to me and my children that morning). I go to a ladies' Bible study. I work with Josh's ministry a lot. During the kids' naptime, I do administrative things, like plan activities, e-mail parents, and work on the website. I lead a Wednesday evening Bible or book study with junior and senior high school girls. I attend Josh's Sunday school class and talk to girls there. I am mainly the youth pastor to the girls, for lack of a better term. I take the phone calls from them, do the discipling, talk at church, take them out to coffee, talk on e-mail and Facebook and MySpace.

"I'm also thinking of starting a Bible study with moms and daughters to try to encourage the communication between parents and teens. And I volunteer at a local women's center, mentoring one girl a week for about one and a half hours."

Jess relinquished her dreams, and God blessed her with exceedingly abundantly more than she could have asked or imagined.

Life on Hold?

Do you ever feel that your life—the life you *really* want—is on hold? While your kiddos are small, should you put your dreams on the shelf to gather dust?

To everything there is a season. We cannot be and do everything all at once. But we can be wonderful mothers and still pursue our dreams. Not full-time, no, but little bits at a time.

We just have to pray for balance—God's balance. We have to carefully weigh every choice we make.

There are no easy answers. I personally think I have the best of both worlds, but that's not always possible for everyone. When I'm struggling with mommy-hood and wishing for something more "exciting," I try to imagine my life without my girls. If I weren't a mom, I'd have all the time in the world to pursue my writing and my hobbies. I could read for hours and hours, devouring piles of books every week. I could travel and learn photography and have the most organized home in the world.

And I'd be a miserable mess—crying my eyes out every day for a baby because I've always wanted to be a mommy.

I dream of writing and speaking and traveling the globe. I dream of family missions trips and sharing book royalties with people in need across the world. I dream of living completely debt free and having someone else clean my home twice a month or so. I dream of meeting fabulous people from all walks of life and all countries of origin. I dream of Gabe quitting his job and pouring his heart into a ministry he loves. I dream of serving my God all day every day with my family.

But I don't want to wish today away. Yes, pursuing all those dreams will be easier when my little ones aren't so little. But I have to build a foundation with them *now* so they'll have the desire to serve Christ when they're older. I don't want to long for the days when my girls are grown and I am "free to do my own thing."

I want to enjoy each moment. I want to live my dream *now*. Sure, it will change and grow and evolve as my family does, but I don't ever want to pursue it at their expense.

I've had to stop and think for a moment. I'm 32 years old and in the prime of my life. This is what I was created to do—to be a mom to little girls. To lay the foundations for them to be godly women and good moms.

Why would I want to wish these days away for more time and freedom? Do I really want my girls to be 16, 14, and 11? Do I want to be in my forties? My fifties?

Don't I want to have something to look forward to? These are the anticipation years—when the best still lies ahead. Isn't that the place I want to be? Where the best is always yet to come? And ironically, that can happen only if I'm having the best time of my life *now*, each day I live bringing more joy than the one before it.

Start Now

I hate to sound like I'm contradicting myself. "Put your kids first!" I tell you. "Start pursuing your dreams now!" I say in the next breath.

It's not a contradiction if you seriously commit every part of your life to the Lord and ask Him to show you that perfect balance. I can't stress that enough, friend. Life is overwhelming. It'll get us every time if we don't surrender it all to God and ask for His perfect wisdom.

We can't do it all. For example, I don't scrapbook. It would overwhelm my life to a point where I couldn't take it. So I've simplified in this area—taking lots of photos and saving mementoes in special boxes and simple books.

Regardless of where you are on the mommy spectrum right now, you can at least be taking baby steps toward a dream.

What might those baby steps look like? Writing down short-term and long-term goals. Looking for ways to cut costs at the grocery store and saving the extra money to put toward your dream. Reading books, doing research. Asking for "dream props" for birthday and Christmas gifts.

We all have creative juices. We all need an outlet for our creativity—a way to express ourselves. Find a friend or group of friends with a similar interest who will encourage you in your pursuit.

For quite a few years now, I've had a passion for helping others pursue *their* passions. I truly believe that when God gives you a light-a-fire-under-me passion for something, He does it for a reason. He intends for you to pursue it on some level. Maybe full-time, maybe not.

God wants His children to find pleasure in serving Him. I'm convinced that if you truly love something, God can help you to use it for His glory. Surely God gives us dreams for a purpose. I think He intentionally plants them in our hearts.

Set your mind to it, and you can do it. If nothing else, you can use those late-night feedings with your tiny one to pray—pray for God's wisdom and blessing as you begin to pursue your dream.

You've just got to start *somewhere*.

At the very least, practice following your dream. It's just like sex. I've said before that when it comes to making time for sex with your hubby, you can't wait until all your kids are in school, or you'll be out of practice and out of touch with your marriage. Same with your dreams. You have to keep in touch with them or they'll fizzle.

I think the ideal situation is to get all your ducks in a row, primed and ready for the moment when your kids no longer need as much of your time. When your little ones become big ones, independent teenagers, you don't want to feel lost, as if you have nothing to do with yourself or your life.

I don't believe the women who tell me, "I'd love to write a book, but I just don't have the time." Neither do I. I wrote my first as a mother of two toddlers, the second while I was pregnant and then nursing a newborn, and the third as a soccer mom with a first grader, a kindergartener, and one still in diapers.

Just do me a favor—don't forget the biggest part of your dream: being a mom.

The Single Passion You Were Made For

Let me leave you with an all-important thought. Following your dreams isn't all about you. It's about God. The awesome thing about God is that when we put Him first, He adds everything back to us. The stuff we thought was so urgent and important often fades in the light of His awesome plan.

He wants us to delight in Him. And our greatest joy in life will be our passion for Christ.

This is the irony of following Christ. Give up your life—and that's when you'll truly live.

"Self-help is no help at all," Jesus says in Luke 9. "Self-sacrifice is the way, my way, to finding yourself, your true self. What good would it do to get everything you want and lose you, the real you?" (verses 24-25 msg).

"God created us to live with a single passion," John Piper says in his book *Don't Waste Your Life*. "To joyfully display his supreme excellence in all the spheres of life. The wasted life is the life without this passion. God calls us to pray and think and dream and plan and work not to be made much of, but to make much of him in every part of our lives."

Strangely enough, according to Jesus, pursuing our dreams isn't the way to find ourselves. Pursuing *Him* is.

And when we pursue Him, our biggest dreams come true.

The Send-Off

At the moment, I'm at Barnes and Noble, sitting in comfy clothes, curled up in an overstuffed chair, sipping a pumpkin spice frappuccino and putting the finishing touches on this book.

Sigh.

I'm looking out over the balcony on the second floor and have a great view of much of the store. The sheer number of books on these shelves overwhelms me. It makes what I'm doing with my life seem so insignificant and small.

Why bother, I wonder. Why bother putting my time and effort, my heart and soul into one little book that will just get lost in the sea of millions and millions of other books that have already been written?

I feel the same way sometimes about being a mom. This is hard. I'm doing a lousy job. And even when I do get something right, it goes unnoticed, unannounced, unappreciated. What meaning does my small life have in the whole great big scheme of things?

We all long to matter. To make a difference. To leave a unique mark on the people whose lives we touch. To change the world.

Yet I am only one person. How can I ever make an impact? I could pound away for years and years without seeing even the tiniest dent.

Oh, friend, God has called us to be faithful, to touch the hearts and lives of the beautiful people He has placed inside our circle of influence regardless of how small that circle may be. To love and encourage and nurture and comfort and help and inspire those people God brings our way.

And it's the smallest people in our circle that matter most. Those precious little beings God has loaned to us while we walk this earth. Can we even comprehend the impact we have on our little ones?

Your child has one mommy—you. No job on earth is more valuable, more honorable, more critical, more significant. It's unparalleled.

God calls some people to change the world in big chunks, some in bite-sized pieces. May we be faithful to follow wherever and however He calls. And may we be joyful and contented when He asks us to change our world one diaper at a time.